Jessica Helfand : Screen

Jessica Helfand : Screen

: Essays on Graphic Design,
: New Media, and Visual Culture

: Princeton Architectural Press

: 2001

⋮

Published by
PRINCETON ARCHITECTURAL PRESS
37 East 7th Street, New York, NY 10003

For a free catalog: 800.722.6657
Web site: www.papress.com

Online companion site to this book:
www.jhwd.com/screen

PRODUCED BY WINTER HOUSE EDITIONS
© 2001 Jessica Helfand. All rights reserved.
Printed and bound in the United States.
04 03 02 01 5 4 3 2 1 FIRST EDITION

"Electronic Typography" and "The Lost Legacy of Film"
originally appeared in *Print Magazine*; "Cult of the
Scratchy" in *The AIGA Journal of Graphic Design*; "Paul
Rand: The Modern Designer" in *The New Republic*;
"Paul Rand: The Modern Professor" in Heller, Steven,
ed., *Paul Rand: A Monograph* (Phaidon Ltd., 1998);
"Sticks and Stones Can Break My Bones" in Blackwell,
Lewis and David Carson, eds., *The End of Print: 2nd
Edition* (Chronicle Books, 2000); all other essays
(except for "The New Illiteracy") appeared in *Eye*.

Library of Congress Cataloging-in-Publication Data
Helfand, Jessica.
Screen: essays on graphic design, new media,
and visual culture / Jessica Helfand.
p. cm.
Includes index.
ISBN 1-56898-310-7
1. Visual communication. 2. Graphic arts. I. Title.
P93.5 .H45 2001
302.23–dc21   2001003629

For Fiona + Malcolm

: Contents

: Contents

: Preface

I have a very early memory of watching television—I was perhaps four at the time—and running to hide under my parents' bed each time the CBS logo flashed boldly upon the screen. The ocular logo, designed in 1951 by William Golden to accompany the Didot letter-forms abbreviating the Columbia Broadcasting System, was a tour-de-force of corporate modernism: simple, spare, and only vaguely anthropomorphic. But to a four-year-old, the vigilant black eyeball was *anything* but vague: it was terrifying. From my concealed lair under the bed it was a huge graphic enemy, static, stoic, and militantly framed in the commanding rectangle of the illuminated screen. In the skewed scale of my toddler perceptions, the eye was as huge as the CBS station identification spot was interminable. I would alternately squeeze my eyes shut, then open them up and try to stare it down.

This was perhaps the first of the many love-hate relationships I have had with screens over the years, from television screens to computer screens to movie screens, PDAS to ATMS, mobile phones to microwave ovens—an infinite series of electronic devices that collectively frame our daily digital peregrinations. Screens surround us; they envelop us; and increasingly, they serve as our primary conduits of information delivery. Their presence in our lives is ubiquitous, seamless, *endless*.

What we see on screen is obviously an issue of considerable importance to communication designers. Are we makers or managers? Controllers or curators? Editors or aesthetes? Perhaps most importantly, to what degree do the classic principles of design—the formal languages, the visual semantics—apply in an environment characterized by randomness and reciprocity, distribution across networks and democracy among netizens? Perhaps one reason John Maeda alludes to Paul Rand in his introduction to this book—and the principal reason my two Rand essays are included in this collection— is that classic design principles do *indeed* apply: it is the *form* their application takes, and the context within which they are articulated that is so critical. (Indeed, Rand's notorious, if seminal influence on a generation of new media and motion graphics designers—from John Maeda to Kyle Cooper—cannot be underestimated.)

Over the past decade, the emergence of the so-called "new" media—dynamic, interactive, and primarily screen-based—has introduced questions of critical importance to designers. These issues affect both the process and the practice of design, raising issues of authorship, craftsmanship, and even citizenship. Indeed, as the lines blur between disciplines and across media, so, too, have the social, geographic, and interpersonal boundaries that once defined discreet aspects of contemporary culture become, in effect, immaterial and meaningless. The process of guiding visual communication, once the principal domain of the graphic designer, is no longer defined by such pristine and quantifiable terms. Rather, it has been co-opted by the participatory functionality that is new media's richest and most enduring asset. The new, contemporary audience is global, fractal, and constantly on the move. And so, it would seem, are we.

The late 1990s proved a period of staggering, unprecedented growth both in new media technologies and the visual phenomena that brought them to life. Such chaos ignited an economic prosperity that developed (and eventually diminished) in parallel to a world in which the designer's relationship to content, context, and audience was to be constantly in flux. Writing about this state of affairs has long been my principal interest: I have written about the woefully misguided myth of Real Time, and examined the fundamental principles of de Stijl as a formal paradigm for rethinking design on the Internet; I have written about the exposition of visual narrative in an environment enhanced by new, time-based choreographic conceits, and about the exposition of recycled narrative given the similarity between mid-twentieth-century TV shows and late-twentieth-century Websites. I have written about silence and about space; about surveillance and about spin; about the birth of alternative models and the death of visual hierarchies in networked environments. I have written about new media and old media, editorial principles and ethical judgments; about memory, manifestoes, and modernity.

Most of the essays in this book were first published between 1994 and 2001 in *Eye Magazine*, in my regular column, *Screen*. The brainchild of *Eye's* founding editor Rick Poynor, *Screen* was initially conceived of as a forum for considering design and new media in a broader social, aesthetic, and cultural context. Our mutual goal was to imagine the screen as a kind of widely understood metaphor both for viewing and for being viewed: the screen itself could be a filter; a frame; a lens; a stage; a mirror or a canvas; a window or a mask; a point of departure or an inescapable destination; a civilization unto itself. Rick gave me the opportunity to mine this polymorphous new territory, to experiment with new ways of looking at, through, and beyond the screen from the kaleidoscopic viewpoints of designer, spectator, and educator; optimist and skeptic; critic and pundit. To date, *Screen* remains a quarterly repository for argument, commentary, and conjecture on all subjects relating to visual media, machine culture, and critical discourse. For providing me with this extraordinary opportunity, I am most grateful to Rick Poynor.

Since Rick's departure from *Eye*, I have had the good fortune to work with Max Bruinsma and John Walters, whose ongoing support I wish to acknowledge here. And for their graceful ability to make me look good in print, I would like to thank Stephen Coates, *Eye's* original design director, and the magazine's current creative visionary, Nick Bell.

My ambitions to publish beyond the design press would not have materialized without Leon Wieseltier, literary editor of *The New*

Republic, whose directive when asking me to write about Paul Rand for a general audience was simply, "Start at the beginning."

My thanks also to David Carson for inviting me to contribute an essay for the second edition of *The End of Print*, and to Fay Weldon, from whose lyrical writings this particular essay is humbly adapted. I am grateful to Martin Fox at *Print Magazine*, who commissioned several of the earlier essays reprinted here. And for his wisdom, knowledge, and graciousness in all matters of editorial collaboration, my thanks to Steven Heller.

I was fortunate to work closely with Paul Rand between 1987 and 1989 when I was a graduate student in Graphic Design at Yale School of Art. Rand was my thesis advisor, an insightful and tireless critic of everything I wrote and how I wrote it. In our conversations, his frequent references to art history, philosophy, and modern art were supported by sources drawn from his substantial library, matched by equally strong opinions about how design, art, and the world all fit together. This intellectual model—at once creative and critical, fueled by observation and fed by intense scrutiny—had an enormous impact on the role writing would later play in my own life. I am deeply appreciative for Mr. Rand's guidance and generosity during those formative years of my education.

I am grateful, too, to many former students and faculty in the Graphic Design program at Yale who generously shared their experiences in the studio with Paul Rand, among them Chris Pullman, whose meticulous archiving of past Rand assignments was matched only by the impeccable documentation of curriculum records recovered for me by Jackie McGuire.

At Princeton Architectural Press, my thanks go to Kevin Lippert for his thoughtful comments and skilled editing. And for his eloquent introduction to this book, my sincerest thanks to John Maeda, Director of the Aesthetics and Computation Group at the MIT Media Lab.

In our studio, I am beholden to our indefatigable research assistant, Eileen Schmidt and to our dedicated designer, Kevin Smith. And of the numerous friends who have lent support, advice, and inspiration I would like to express particular thanks to my oldest friend, Martha Goldhirsh.

And finally, a note of thanks to my family: to my parents, William and Audrey Helfand; to my beautiful children, Malcolm and Fiona; and most of all, to my husband and partner, William Drenttel—my dearest and most devoted friend.

FALLS VILLAGE, CONNECTICUT
JULY 2001

: Infinite Loops
John Maeda

My first encounter with a personal computer was twenty years ago in a math classroom during junior high school. At the time, it was never clear to any of us what it might be useful for, beyond the literal act of "using the computer." But "using a computer" meant only the passive act of sitting in front of the computer to stare at a small blinking green rectangle. The secret hope was that it would entertain you with loud graphics and sound like its close relative, the television. But such bliss never came and we were driven to interact with the device through its tiny keyboard. However, anything we typed, whether a name, a happy thought, and even things not as dear, would be evaluated by the computer with great insignificance. "SYNTAX ERROR," it would retort.

I surely would never have advanced beyond the foyer of computer programming if it were not for my well-to-do classmate, who, as evidence of his absurd wealth, had a similar unit at home! He showed me how to teach the computer to say my name with a simple statement like "PRINT 'MAEDA'." The computer would dutifully reply, "MAEDA." With a few more instructions the computer would repeat my name twice, fifty times, on to a hundred, and then practically forever. The implication of this simple mechanism of repetition, by which the computer was clearly king, was further dramatized when we hooked the computer to a printer. The printer would print and print until all of its paper supply was consumed, still hungry for more. Upon seeing this and similar displays of the printer's athleticism and waste, my instructor would shout disapprovingly, "No infinite loops allowed!" Only a subsequent command to terminate the processing flow, the chording of two keys on the keyboard, would stop the madness.

Surely, my instructor would disapprove of the situation we face today with computers of the twenty-first century. From the very moment its electronic soul ignites at the touch of the power button, the computer drags you into an infinite loop of "yes-no-cancel" queries that hints at our future existence as a species requiring only one finger for clicking and a brain as optional hardware accessory.

The common acceptance of the term "computer user" to describe our daily relationship with computers hides a fundamental philosophical question. Are we the users of the computers, or are the computers using us? In the complex infinite loops of today's highly interactive software, how far could a computer go without our constant tending to its incessant needs to confirm its manner of being? Were we to let it go along its infinite ways without any need for human input, would we know which keys to press to terminate the madness?

Screen: Essays on Graphic Design, New Media, and Visual Culture is an account of one artist's attempts to cope with the onslaught of technology by reacting with a graceful, literary paintbrush. Through a score of thoughtful essays developed over a decade, Jessica Helfand reveals herself as someone who has freely stepped out of the firing range of new media developments in order to vent her perspective as therapies of text. Jessica skillfully exercises a vast vocabulary of art historical and philosophical references that will be of vital importance to the student of new media by providing valuable perspectives, both academic and personal. An example of this most personal viewpoint is exhibited in her two deeply entertaining essays on Paul Rand, a mentor that both Jessica and I share. These two essays alone are reasons enough to need this book.

In the swirling, upgradable, commodified, and impersonal world of the technologies that coming generations will face, our only hope for meaningful survival will be a salvation based upon strong personal voices. Witness the demise just in the last decade of the super-designer class of Müller-Brockmann, Rand, Kamekura, and Munari. In their wake we have the latest "boys-band" and other rock-star crazes of design, only recently replaced by an economic somberness that will surely serve to codify and deify the surprisingly few advances that have been made in the name of digital. The body of work that Jessica represents in this book I would classify as neither digital nor anti-digital. It is personal, passionate, and hopeful—which will ultimately inspire you to become better, whatever that may mean.

This essay examines ways in which time itself is visualized and critiques the pronounced emphasis on acceleration that typifies contemporary culture. Looking at analogous models, historical antecedents, and parallel disciplines—from late-nineteenth-century parlor games to early twentieth-century radio broadcasts—the intersections of lifestyle, time progression, and human interaction are discussed with an eye to understanding what it is that makes time real at all.

: One, Two, Three, *Faux:*
The Myth of Real Time

Lewis Mumford once wrote that he believed the industrial age was merely a passing phase in which the quality of human life would be sacrificed to further the prowess of technology. In contemporary culture, technology's legacy—and Mumford's prophecy—do indeed suggest a society utterly transfixed by its passion for speed. And most ironically in our impatient electronic culture, the phrase "Real Time" has come to symbolize the instantaneous, the nanosecond, or, what distinguished media oracle Marshall McLuhan once referred to as "allatonceness." Today, as we struggle to reconcile the virtual against the tangible, what does it mean to be real at all?

As it is, there is nothing particularly real at all about Real Time, and certainly nothing human about it. In electronic media, where the transmittal of data depends upon the generally unreliable support of varying bandwidth, Real Time is immediate time, everything at once time, time without interruption or delay. Real Time implies no waiting—but in the Real World, don't we occasionally wait for things? We wait in supermarket lines, at the bank, in movie queues; we wait "on hold" on the telephone, or put the VCR on "pause" to answer the door. Information transmittal, whether on CD-ROM or via networked phone lines or in face-to-face conversation, takes time. Delays, whether momentary or extended, are the casualties of such unpredictable transmittals and mirror the very real delays we face in everyday life. "Historical time is intermittent and variable," notes George Kubler in *The Shape of Time,* suggesting quite reasonably that indeed, life happens in between those moments. For electronic experiences to resonate with equal meaning, it would seem imperative for such lapses to be duly recognized, if not celebrated altogether.

Time takes many forms, and not all of them are real. There is psychological time, perceptual time, imaginary time, spiritual time. Social psychologists have observed that reality is made up of an amalgam of all of these. Noted sociologist P. A. Sorokin once observed that each culture and discipline has its own perception of time and its meaning: his definition of socio-cultural time is a conceptual model that lacks the distinguishing characteristics of horological time, instead using points of reference that are determined by unique social conditions. The irregular ebb and flow of time as it parallels human experience is a rich pattern marked by speed as well as slowness. By definition, the multifaceted nature of this concept prevents us from adopting a singular model for understanding the shape of time.

But by equating "real" with "efficient" we mistakenly perpetuate the idea that acceleration is the principal goal not only of performance, but of life itself. In so doing, we minimize both the value of human interaction and the potential for design to mediate that interaction. Real Time, in this context, is a misnomer: a more worthy definition comes from cognitive psychologist Donald Norman, who rightly observes that "real time is what humans do."

Like the concentric rings that indicate the age of a tree, the course of time takes many forms. Typically, we have come to recognize and respond to the kinds of visual codes that depict the gradual passage of time. While it takes only a fraction of a second to take a photograph, for example, the reverse side of a print from a photo library is stamped each time it is requested for publication, revealing, over time, a rich texture that bespeaks its long, productive life. Imagine if it were possible to build texture such as this in email, or over the Internet, or as a consequence of one's participation in a chatroom. Yet as long as digital is understood to be ephemeral, the genesis of an idea—and its very rich evolution over time—will be impossible to visualize in quite the same manner.

Fake Time—or time as it currently exists—implies slower time. The implication here is that it is sluggish, retarded, anathema to the very acceleration that characterizes technological achievement in the twentieth century. Why is this non-instantaneous time not perceived of as reflective time? Or thoughtful time? Or quality time? Writing half a century ago of their disenchantment with the high-velocity life, poets such as T. S. Eliot and William Carlos Williams lamented the lack of tranquility and leisure in the face of emerging industry. Today, leisure itself has become such a rare commodity that it is deemed an area worthy of serious sociological inquiry—an anachronistic relic of our lost culture.

The visualization of time itself has always challenged designers, perhaps because the very unpredictability of its character precludes its being pummeled into any finite shape. And yet, for centuries humans have been trying to rationalize time, to harness it into a form at once controllable and clear. Since the fourteenth century, the civilized world has measured time by the 24-hour clock. Agricultural societies and less technologically sophisticated cultures have typically operated in a similar manner, relying instead on the natural but highly regulatory movements of the planets. The seven-day calendar takes its cues from the movements of these celestial bodies, as the seven principal planets—beginning with the Sun and ending with Saturn—still provide the English (and French) speaking world with the etymological basis for its naming conventions. Human time-keeping systems are equally cyclical, if less apparently so: sleep rhythms and metabolic balances are as predictable as seasonal changes. Like the cycles that characterize planetary phenomena, such conditions can neither be anticipated, nor precipitated, nor accelerated at will.

While our current systems for mapping time have their roots in the Egyptian solar calendar, the rationalization of time that has come to characterize the modern world has evolved over numerous centuries and across multiple cultures. As a tool for managing time, the calendar itself offers a tabular system of temporal subdivision, enabling the rational and lateral compartmentalization of time. Seeing our weeks laid out in front of us, the assumption is that we can better control our time. Ironically, the great failure of the calendar lies in the homogeneity of its basic form: Monday is the same shape as Saturday, and June looks just like December. As the physical embodiment of this rationalization, the Filofax celebrates this efficiency by chopping time up into more digestible subdivisions, thus allowing us to conceptualize our days in "at-a-glance" modules of mornings or meetings or "to do" lists. Add to this the hyper-efficiency of electronic calendars and time management software, and time looks to be careening by even faster than the last time you checked.

Conversely, in time-based media the serendipity we pretend to enjoy is buried in a calculated process where all the permutations have been anticipated in advance. It is time-based because it is dynamic, but can it ever mirror the magical unpredictability and believable rhythms of real life? The basic economics of making interactive products depends to a considerable degree upon the technological wizardry of compression: speedy downloads are looked upon more favorably because they save us time, but the hidden danger here lies in truncating an experience as a consequence of so doing.

This urge to race through information may explain why so much of the metaphor and visualization in new media takes its cue from game culture. Woefully overlooked here are strategic games—chess, for example—that historically have had much more to do with human interaction and the speed with which such interaction naturally takes place. A better model might lie in the parlor games of the nineteenth century, board games and puzzles that were played at a slower and, indeed, a more social pace. To date, such games demand a kind of reflective time which, though very real for those engaging in such activities, remains virtually ignored in the race to achieve Real Time nirvana.

Overlooked, too, are previous examples that successfully merged technology and society, addressing issues of social harmony and community interaction. Radio broadcasts half a century ago engaged and united audiences around boxes with plugs connecting them to an outlet in the wall. All radios did was deliver information electronically: they were tools for social congregation, valuable for their ability to disseminate a signal across the globe. But listening even today to the voices of Roosevelt and Churchill reminds us that the signal drew its real meaning from the rich cadences and intonation of the politicians themselves. Time compression would not have helped in the least: yet today, as we channel-chase and net-surf across the digital landscape, we are under the mistaken notion that we are richer for the experience of doing so.

Time itself is unquestionably our richest and most imperiled resource, underscoring everything we do and see and feel. If McLuhan was correct in his assumption that technologies achieve purpose when they extend humanity throughout the world, then our relentless pursuit of speed seems an illogical method for doing so. It is perhaps his more pragmatic observation that instantaneous electronic communication results in noticeable social disturbances that demands our immediate consideration: for designers, this means taking the time to rethink ways of visualizing messages to engage new and increasingly complex audiences.

Remarkably, studies of visual perception have found that two-dimensional images projected onto the retina only achieve full dimensionality as a result of our perception: we infer the third dimension of depth. Sadly, though, as the urgency to expedite all communicative transactions usurps our customary patterns of exchange, perception is accelerated as well. There does not seem to be a great deal of time left over to infer—or interpret, or imagine—much of anything at all. In the end, of course, there is nothing real about this at all, except for our propensity to let it happen.

As the screen becomes a stage upon which media of all kinds must perform, our collective cultural experience of watching television offers innumerable cues for deciphering the alleged innovations of contemporary media. This essay debunks the notion that computer media is new media, and identifies ten precursors in television—from talk shows (the precursors of chatrooms) to channel chasing (surfing) to escapist situation comedies (virtual online habitats) and serialized soap operas (hyperlinked narratives)—to show that television did it first.

: Television Did It First:
Ten Myths about "New" Media

In 1934, the American biologist William Beebe descended into a bathysphere to a depth of 3,028 feet—a record at the time. While his journey was widely reported on radio, today this historic event remains all but forgotten, trapped in the technology of its time. And so it goes, as radio's coverage of the bathysphere is replaced by television's coverage of the biosphere, supplanted by the Web's 62-minute global coverage of our most recent total lunar eclipse. Will television soon become a forgotten relic now that the Web is here?

Unlikely. Yet in discussions of new media, television is rarely—if ever—cited. If and when it is, it is granted a kind of nostalgic mention: in the summer of 1996, a *New York Times* reporter commented that, given its remarkable coverage of the Mars landing, the Web had finally come into its own as a popular news medium, "just as the broadcast of John F. Kennedy's assassination became the defining moment for television as the nation's information conduit of choice." This is but one of many examples of the ways in which television, as a distribution mechanism capable of capturing the immediacy of global experience, likens itself to the Web.

But television did it first.

As a mutable, unpredictable, and increasingly complex cultural ideal, "experience" has never been easy to capture, perhaps least of all by designers. (And if I hear one more designer say, "but what I really want to do is to design experiences," I think I will scream. One is immediately reminded of the unemployed actor who swears that what he really wants to do is direct.) Nonetheless, as the screen becomes a stage upon which media of all kinds must perform, one could argue that our collective cultural experience of watching television offers innumerable cues for deciphering the alleged innovations of contemporary media.

It is still easier to watch TV; it is also perhaps more efficient to surf the Web, given the specificity with which search engines allow us to plot the minutiae of our own course. Conversely, interactivity—as a two-way medium—provides perhaps a greater feeling of personal reward than the inert TV viewer might experience. And there is, too, the very basic fact that the installed base of couches still greatly overshadows the number of personal computers in general circulation. Most puzzling, however, the prevailing sentiment seems to celebrate the new at the expense of the old. And what is so new about new media, anyway? Herewith, a few myths debunked:

MYTH 01: The Internet makes everyone a star.
FACT: Television game shows did it first.
Game shows, quiz shows—people will do anything to be on television, to publicize the silly or sordid details of their own lives, and, to the great delight of the viewing public, to degrade themselves wildly in the process. The Web services this very affliction by empowering users with a kind of *carte blanche* for rampant self-expression: everyone has a Webpage, everyone has an opinion, everyone is a star.

MYTH 02: Virtual reality invites us to escape normal reality.
FACT: "Escapist" situation comedies did it first.
In the United States, the 1960s saw a preponderance of comedies produced for television dominated by themes related to magic, witchcraft and fantasy. The popularity of shows like "I Dream of Jeannie" (a genie living in a bottle); "Bewitched" (a witch living in suburbia); "Mr. Ed" (a talking horse) or "My Mother the Car" (a talking car) lay in a slapstick formula that was repeated successfully again and again. In a decade of enormous political upheaval and social change, viewers found respite in watching—and indeed, in identifying with—characters who were at once unthreatening (mother's always in the garage) and clever (how did Jeannie manage to get out of that safe?). Now fast-forward some 30-odd years: consider the creation of virtual worlds we can invent—and inhabit—on the Web. No longer limited by the physical restrictions of the terrestrial world, such alternative environments fuel our imagination and encourage escape. But in today's decidedly less turbulent political climate, just what is it we are escaping from? Devotees of new media claim today's interactive technologies offer immersive experiences: yet while empowering, the capacity for immersion is still dependent upon innumerable variables—connection speed, monitor settings, entering a URL with no typos—that it

remains a distant, if intangible ideal. The Web works best as a kind of giant database, helping us manage the information jungle that threatens to overwhelm us. In this view, television still seems an easier escape from reality.

MYTH 03: Content online should always play to the user's abbreviated attention span.
FACT: TV viewers have always had a short attention span: variety and "vignette" television did it first.
Comic variety shows such as "Laugh In" and "Saturday Night Live" in the U.S., and "Benny Hill" and "Monty Python" in the U.K., have long been popular, crafted with the impatient viewer in mind. Banter characterized by brevity, pithy one-liners and exaggerated double-takes are a few of the devices that serve this genre well: on TV, they become the entry points for the channel-chasing viewer. On the Web, such percussive dialogue is the fabric of email: to channel-chase is to surf, an equally if not more impatient activity.

MYTH 04: "New" media must be kinetic in order to hook users.
FACT: Broadcast news television did it first.
In an interview in 1997, "Sixty Minutes" Executive Producer Don Hewitt described his secret for engaging an audience. "You must have action in the first twelve seconds," he said. "It doesn't matter what the action is." The show, a legend in network news television, has won sixty-eight Emmy awards since its inception in 1968 and is the longest continuously-running primetime program ever. (Four years later, in an unusual display of moral conscience, Hewitt acknowledged his complicity in spawning this questionable genre. In his memoir *Tell Me a Story: Fifty Years and 60 Minutes in Television,* Hewitt apologizes for having fathered a form that has since gone horribly awry. Referring to the slippery slope of truth and drama referred to above, Hewitt writes: "We ruined television because we made it so profitable to do this kind of thing.") Certainly this blanket concept, whether intended as a definition of good television (or worse, of good journalism) raises critical questions about the credibility of these shows in general. Does such emphasis on action slant the reporting of news? Is our attention span as a viewing public so short that we need to see things

constantly moving in order to to stay awake? Have we been so indoc-trinated by the lure of action films and crime shows that we yearn to see such dramas unfold in the telling of our nightly news? The degree to which design conspires to build impact—whether through special effects or creative editing techniques—lies at the core of this debate: is "action" merely news made visually manifest? If so, what is the creative role for design? What is the ethical role?

MYTH 05: Reality TV is a new programming genre: it is all about voyeurism.
FACT: Reality TV has been around since the 1950s. Voyeurism has been around even longer.
Nostalgia buffs may recall a television series in both Britain and the U.S. entitled "This is Your Life" which, beginning in the mid-50s, was modeled on the following "Reality TV" model: an unsuspecting celebrity was accosted by a TV host (Eammon Edwards in the U.K.; Ralph Edwards in the U.S.;) and made to publicly endure a retelling of his or her life, in front of a live studio audience, through the surprise appearance of various guests who would share their memories of the subject in question. Unrehearsed and impromptu, the show was a mixture of pulpy nostalgia and pure humiliation. (In England, Football star Danny Blanchflower reportedly walked off the set in a stormy public display of embarrassment and anger at the invasion of his per-sonal privacy.)

Today's Reality TV offerings ("Survivor," "Big Brother," "The Weakest Link" among others) differ only in their candor: rather than try to conceal the invasion of privacy, they celebrate it. Participants "share" information that results in exposing the flaws of their oppo-nents, rather than applauding their charms. Clearly, the Internet in general (and Webcams in particular) go to great lengths to facilitate a kind of virtual voyeurism that is simply an updated variant of "This is Your Life" with greater shock value—but without the celebrity status.

MYTH 06: Hyperlinked storytelling allows for interconnected narratives.
FACT: Television (and radio) soap operas did it first.
The dramatic genre known broadly as the soap opera depends on a formula of serialized storytelling that has its own pace, unfolding

steadily over weeks and months, spawning iterative, obstreperous links to other characters, stories, and occasionally to entire other shows. Character-driven rather than plot-based, soaps quickly become hyperlinked mini-orbits of interconnected people and places, threaded narratives and stories with no endings.

These programs ("EastEnders," "Guiding Light") succeed largely for two reasons: first, because they build viewer interest steadily over time and across multiple plot lines (if you don't like one story you're sure to like another) and second, because the cumulative effect of this kind of viewing has a kind of residual emotional value: it succeeds not because it is physically interactive (click that mouse!) but because it is behaviorally interactive (tune in tomorrow!). Unlike the mathematically-plotted hyperlinks in many digital narratives where the emphasis is on action (think *Myst*), soaps succeed precisely because of this underlying emotional pull.

MYTH 07: Real-Time transmissions on the Web allow users to "experience" history in the making.
FACT: Edward R. Murrow did it first.
Reporting daily on the radio from London during the Blitz and several years later (with the support of the then "new" coaxial cable) on television, Murrow made history in the early 1950s by transmitting his reports to both American coasts at once. Premiering in 1951, his 30-minute news program, "See It Now" opened with Murrow seated at a table, the camera pulling back to show parallel live shots of the Statue of Liberty in New York and the Bay in San Francisco. "We are impressed," he declared solemnly, "by a medium through which a man sitting in his living room has been able to look at both oceans at once." Recent Webcasts (24 Hours in Cyberspace, the chess match between Kasparov and Big Blue) are really no different; yet ironically, we remain perpetually amazed by such experiments in broadcast simultaneity.

MYTH 08: Online chatrooms offer a new way to promote social interaction and build community.
FACT: Television talk shows did it first.
The television talk-show format lets viewers watch as an informal dialogue unfolds between interviewer and interviewee(s), the studio

audience and the occasional telephone caller. Online chats and threaded discussions do the same: in each medium, there is a tendency toward idiosyncratic topics, a frequent and generally unpredictable splintering of themes, and a sort of uneditable and messy, down-home energy. The more formatted they become, the less modulation there is among voices, or visuals, or the "experiences" these dialogues (or "multilogues") generate. Most talk show sets look alike, as do most online discussions. Chatland ... or flatland?

MYTH 09: Web advertising is annoying. Why can't someone make those banners go away?
FACT: TV advertising is annoying. Why can't someone make those commercials go away?

MYTH 10: The lure of selection draws people to surf the Web.
FACT: Television, in all its multi-channel glory, did it first.
It is perhaps ironic that the same things we celebrate about new media are the things we once said we hated about TV. Quantity instead of quality. Edutainment instead of education. Media saturation. Privacy invasion. With satellites and syndication, cable and now the Web, the selection (of channels, of sites) expands; the price (of hardware, of software) diminishes while the input device (remote, mouse) continues to permit steady steering and increased navigation. (Incidentally, the remote has been around since 1955.)

And what of our media addiction? In 1996, *Newsweek* reported that by the age of two, American kids spend an average of twenty-seven hours per week in front of the TV. Now add time spent Websurfing, and there is precious little time left to go froggin' down by the creek. Will the alleged "merger" of Web and TV help minimize this frightening statistic?

Ironically, our dreams of a new hybrid medium are likely to reveal just the opposite: the survival of one medium over the other. Which will it be? Unlike TV, the good news about the Web is that is helps us see things in more digestible portions: critical mass, that terrifying notion of yesteryear, has given way to more rational ideas about community and identity; about hierarchy and chronology; and about efficiency, clarity, and accessibility. The bad news is, such fragmentation isolates individuals and creates a kind of lonely and disenfranchised—if empowered—user. And even this idea of the empowered user is (at least conceptually) not a new one. It was, after all, David Ogilvy who—more than twenty-five years ago—wrote: "The consumer is not a moron: she's your wife."

What we know is that today's media audiences expect the speed and performance of TV, with the functionality and scope of the Web. They want to be lazy and they want to be engaged. They are users, viewers, and readers; senders and receivers; the judge and the jury. And it is only going to get more complicated as these lines continue to blur: between WWW and TV; between VDT and VCR; between static media, time-based media, and merged media. Call it what you will, but none of it is new.

This essay, written in the didactic prose style of the manifesto, is a rant. Its goal is to debunk the exalted claims of wannabe philosophers and soap-box proselytizers, to critique the posturing and the pretense, the lofty promises, the loose-cannon platitudes. It applauds original thinking and admonishes cheap shots. It supports the intrinsic merits of personality and skewers the implausible motives of "personalization." It commends modernism, where appropriate, and critiques marketing, where not. It tries to acknowledge the authentic (what's progress?), to identify the artificial (what's plagiarism?) and to illuminate the difference between the two.

: Me, the Undersigned

What is it about the manifesto that stirs us so? Defined as "a public declaration of principles or intentions,"[1] manifestoes have been penned for centuries to decry injustice or to define truth, to denounce authority or to restore faith—even to rethink purpose and reassess value. In practice, the modern manifesto seems mostly to combine idealistic wishlists with idiosyncratic value judgments: buried somewhere in there is a kind of implicit kernel of protest, but what exactly do these manifestoes protest *against,* the reader wonders? Such solemn proclamations of opinion—sheer moral outrage masquerading as factual observations—have their modern roots in early twentieth-century art movements whose advocates managed to wax poetic while at the same time, rallying their troops for revolt. There was the Cubist Manifesto, ("The time has come for us to be the masters," wrote Guillaume Apollinaire in 1913) and five years later, the Dada Manifesto ("Every man must shout," wrote Tristan Tzara. "There is great destructive, negative work to be done."). André Breton "hurled formal warnings to society" in his impassioned 1925 Surrealist Manifesto, while Filippo Tommaso Marinetti dubbed his own 1913 Futurist Manifesto "incendiary," as he preached a celebration of danger (glorify war!), a renunciation of classicism (destroy the museums!) and a radical redefinition of beauty that scorned women, endorsed aggression, and embraced artistic freedom at all costs.[2] To read Marinetti now, nearly one hundred years later and outside the turbulent political climate in which he was originally intended to be read, is to understand fervor as a basic operating principle—and arguably, to consider some of the more fatuous promises of the digital age in an entirely new light.[3]

The tempestuous era framing the pronouncements of early modernist doctrine is, of course, long gone. In its wake, postmodernists seem to have comparatively dispassionate views: they simply refuse to take anything very seriously. ("While modernism thrived on multiple manifestoes," explains *The New York Times* cultural critic Edward Rothstein, "postmodernism's manifesto might be that no manifesto is possible.") So how to explain its sudden return? Art movements aside and fascist tendencies notwithstanding, the manifesto, in its purest incarnation, is still largely considered a powerful purveyor of ideology; by conjecture, it is also a provocative social stimulant for self-appointed activists. Activism itself can be a potent motive for putting pen to paper, and it is likely that the modern-day activist's tactical advantage lies in mastering the art of such pointedly dogmatic prose. It is precisely this imperiousness, this preachiness that sets it apart from everything else we read: from the Cluetrain Manifesto ("Hyperlinks subvert hierarchy") to David Gelernter's Second Coming Manifesto ("Computing will be transformed") to Bruce Mau's Incomplete Manifesto for Growth ("Ask stupid questions") to the First Things First Manifesto ("We propose a reversal of priorities")[4] to the Dogma Manifesto ("We propose a vow of chastity") to the New Puritans Manifesto ("We believe in grammatical purity") to the U.N. 2000 Peace Manifesto ("Respect all life") to the Unabomber Manifesto (just under 35,000 words about why we *shouldn't* respect life and, well, enough said).

Actually, not nearly enough said. There are hundreds, even thousands of manifestoes in general circulation, and it would not be an overstatement to suggest that the great majority of these are eminently forgettable, unabashedly self-aggrandizing, or just plain tiresome in their pandering attempts to define What Is Important: consider, for example, the Simplicity Manifesto ("Simplicity is power!") or the Internet Manifesto ("No information shall be censored!"). There are manifestoes written to oppose pretty much anything: like the Squash the TV Bugs Manifesto, which vociferously rejects the overuse of what its advocates call "Obnoxicons," (the faux blind-embossed, semi-transparent network identification logos that reside in the corners of TV screens). There are even manifestoes written to oppose manifestoes, such as the Anti-Manifesto ("What's the matter with kids today?"[5]) and the Anti-Anti Manifesto ("The First Amendment isn't an excuse for ignorance.").

Conversely, it is the rare but delightful manifesto that combines original insights with welcome doses of irony: I am thinking here of P. J. O'Rourke's Clinton-bashing Liberty Manifesto ("There is only one basic human right: the right to do as you damn well please.") or Karrie Jacobs' modernist-bashing Fruitbowl Manifesto ("Perfection is intimidating. You have to be on your best behavior to live with it."). To be fair (and historically accurate) manifestoes on topics of universally acknowledged importance—civil jurisprudence and nuclear disarmament, for example—have been written in the interests of reducing confusion, consolidating opinion, or securing widespread consensus. Documents such as these are not only initially relevant, but also accumulate added value over time. (A good example is the Bertrand Russell/Albert Einstein 1955 Manifesto that laid the foundations for the modern peace movement.)

In general, though, the philosophical tenets upon which so many modern manifestoes lay their claims often seem inflated, invented, or simply self-serving. And what better medium to promote such exploits than the World Wide Web? As a publishing platform, it is uniquely positioned to both display and distribute the gospel according to anybody-who-wants-to-volunteer-an-opinion. The Web is a maelstrom of rampant self-expression: a First-Amendment free-for-all. (On the up side, networked culture is also devoid of such interpersonal perils as oppression, hierarchy, domination, and exclusivity. It is socially non-sectarian: an anti-proletariat.) This "reading" of the Internet as a kind of natural habitat for self-publishing is precisely what encourages so much impassioned writing. In truth, and beyond its claims of efficiency and progress, the Web's facility for networked data exchange supports a kind of hopelessly reciprocal social infrastructure that has become an unusually fertile breeding ground for the manifesto. Funny that the social equalities presumed possible on the Web have themselves spawned such didacticism—with its overtones of moral superiority, its artistic idealism, its philosophical imperatives. And it is precisely this kind of didacticism—the world according to me, me, me—that has, in a sense, become the Web's *lingua franca*.

At the core of this not insignificant cultural paradigm shift lies the Internet itself, a broad and still largely undefined social platform that levels the playing field to such an extent that we no longer know where we stand—or what, more importantly, we stand *for.* Enter the manifesto: preaching to the converted, the non-converted, whoever will listen. Bearing in mind the limited attention span of the general public, the typical contemporary manifesto is pithy, abbreviated, and strident in tone, a staccato series of ex-cathedra statements and, it is hoped, quote-worthy sound bytes. Here is the basic formula, as I see it: Take an idea. Break it down into its component parts. (Write short sentences: think *doctrinaire.)* Add paragraph breaks. Bullets. Numbers. Now add Lots! Of! Punctuation! Assume everyone on the planet will agree with you and proceed to express yourself with the much-anticipated collective enthusiasm of the madding crowds. Upload keywords. And post! If you are feeling unsure about any of this, get a few friends together and coerce them into adding their names to your list of lofty ideals: "We, the undersigned" means if your ship goes down, you are not the only one on board.

This being an election year in the U.S. and the start of a new century, it seems somehow appropriate that I take a stab at writing my own manifesto. Surprising as it may seem to my loyal readers, I have no particular political ideology or aesthetic bias or subversive agenda to proclaim, no prevailing morality to preach or aggrieved practices to denounce. There are no signatories to this manifesto— or, as a very wise friend of mine is fond of saying, "my views do not represent anyone but me."

My manifesto is a rant. It is intended to debunk the exalted claims of wannabe philosophers and soap-box proselytizers, to critique the posturing and the pretense, the lofty promises, the loose-cannon platitudes. My manifesto applauds original thinking and admonishes cheap shots. It supports the intrinsic merits of personality and it skewers the implausible motives of "personalization." It commends modernism, where appropriate, and critiques marketing, where not. It tries to acknowledge the authentic (what's progress?), to identify the artificial (what's plagiarism?) and to illuminate the difference between the two. Its goal is to cut through the clutter and rebuke the rhetoric, to reconsider some of the ideas that really matter—at least to me.

Then again, my views do not represent anyone but me.

MANIFESTO™

01. Information architecture is not architecture.

02. Empowerment is not the same as entitlement.

03. Personalization is not the same as personality.

04. Convergence remains more successful in concept than in execution.

05. The proliferation of mysterious acronyms is inversely proportionate to the number of original ideas in the world.

06. The installed base of couches still overshadows the number of personal computers in general circulation.

07. Less is a chore.

08. The killer app never killed anybody.

09. Faster is not the same as better.

10. Space is not the final frontier.

ANNOTATIONS TO THE MANIFESTO

01. Six years ago, Clement Mok took the stage at a New York AIGA business conference and proposed the term "information architect" as a more accurate title for what most graphic designers—especially those engaged in new and complex media—do for a living. My view then was the same as now: as long as we are choosing new titles, I would like to change mine to "brain surgeon." Much as we would prefer to think otherwise, design, unlike architecture (and for that matter, brain surgery) remains an industry in which one need not—indeed, cannot—be certified to practice. Architecture is architecture, information be damned. What we design, as novel and revolutionary as it might seem at the time of our designing it, is still just design. Simply stated: Graphic design is probably not going to kill you if it falls on your head.

02. In a talk several years ago at the Cato Institute (a nonpartisan public policy research foundation in Washington, D.C.) author and sometime political pundit P. J. O'Rourke remarked: "Freedom is not empowerment. Empowerment is what the Serbs have in Bosnia." Freedom of expression (an issue of some consequence to manifesto-writers) is a constitutional right, but in extreme cases—the Unabomber Manifesto, for example—free expression becomes forcible terrorism and the consequences are lethal. At the same time, the relationship between the autonomies which such "freedoms" can provide through technology (long-distance learning, for example) and one's empowerment in pursuing such opportunities (a college degree, for example) contribute to a sense of exalted personal entitlement: If anybody can get a Harvard degree online, then why not me? (If anybody can get a Harvard degree online, then what is to become of Harvard?) It is easy to see how quickly (and inappropriately) empowerment contributes to our sense of entitlement: but while both share a certain quality of warped fetishism (one is fed by illusions of digitally enhanced grandeur; the other, by distorted perceptions of privilege) they are *not* interchangeable.

03. The advent of customized everything may well contribute to the entitlement vs. empowerment debate, but is of particular concern to issues of privacy. "Personality" is what makes you special. "Personalization" telegraphs the illusion that you are special: yet to enable technologies to customize your profile is to expose your identity, streamline your personality, and ultimately jeopardize the very privacy that is your most inalienable right. "Personality" is to "unique" what "personalization" is to "universal." "Personalization" means you have submitted information that enables you to be tracked: it is a front for surveillance that lets you be repackaged as a "you" that is a distributable demographic statistic. Personally, I am waiting for someone to offer customizable encryption software that lets me be *me*. The Electronic Privacy Information Center claims to offer an array of tools that protect such privacies through email—from "snoop-proof" mail applications to virtual paper shredders. (For more on the status of privacy policies, and the availability of these resources, see: www.epic.org/privacy/tools.html.)

04. Though it promises the kind of seamless integration we have imagined since the dawn of the Industrial Revolution, convergence remains largely a myth. The phrase "out of the box" (the wireless dream of convergent hopefuls) is equally problematic. Yet what remains critical—and largely unresolved—are the economic imperatives that drive not only the manufacture of our digital devices, but more importantly, their inevitable consumption. Beyond the perils of monopolization (as seen, for instance, in the protracted two-year well-publicized antitrust suit against Microsoft) there are compelling arguments for the enduring value of "healthy" competition. (For more on the relationship between convergence and stagnation, see: www.convergence.org/info/faq.html.)

05. In the days of Marx and Marinetti, manifestoes were passionately scripted: adorned with flowery or extreme language, punctuated with inflammatory suggestion, filled with mixed metaphor and near-hallucinogenic word pictures. By contrast, today's offerings are skimpy and forcibly restrained—even brusque. To what do we owe this seismic shift in style? Is terse language a consequence of modernist reduction, streamlined sentences mirroring the formal economy of, say, synthetic plastics? Are punchy, bulleted "tips" more likely to seize a reader's attention, given the likelihood that s/he is already under attack by a veritable deluge of information? Contemporary manifesto-speak has supplanted lyrical prose with generic jargon: we think we sound smarter when we abbreviate with such concocted acronyms, but in reality, the opposite is more likely to be true: In the entire lexicon of universally-accepted new media jargon, the acronym is the most annoying component. Beyond "eyeballs" and "drill-downs," beyond "action items" and "affinity groups" and "data mining" lie a conspiracy of enigmatic abbreviations, of "KPI(s)" and "CSF(s)" (key performance indicators and critical success factors); "users" (read people) are evaluated for their "LMS" (lifestyle management services) and "mindshare" (read products) analyzed for their "UBV" (unique brand value). All of these "HRS" (human resource strategies) are, of course, intended to maximize saturation opportunities for BRANDING—a concept that to me, instantly conjures up images of cattle being torched on the belly by a very hot iron.

06. According to a report published in 2000 by the Annenberg Public Policy Center, low-income families (defined as those with an income of less than $30,000 per year) are much less likely to have computers, or Internet access, or newspaper subscriptions compared with their middle income ($30,000–$75,000 per year) and high income (over $75,000 per year) counterparts. Of all the media surveyed, children spend the most time with television, over two hours per day (147 minutes). They spend the least time per day on the Internet (14 minutes per day).

07. I remain firmly convinced that good designers are good editors. This means having not only the instinct, but a willingness to commit that instinct—a sense of conviction—to articulate why one choice is preferable to another. Editing, like much of the reductivist thinking that characterizes classic design education, suggests a kind of basic working methodology that not only shapes formal decisions, but also informs conceptual ones. It is a pretty simple equation: just say *no*. And yet, in this age of more-better-faster, never before has something so simple been so hard to communicate. In the area of online publishing, this is an especially precarious issue: just because you can do or say or publish or design something, must you? Is less better? Not necessarily. But it certainly seems harder to come by. The plea for a pared-down ideal, however, is not unique to the design disciplines: similar core values are proposed, for example, in the Dogma Manifesto, published "in the hope of rescuing world cinema from decadent bourgeois individualism" by Danish filmmakers Lars von Trier and Thomas Vinterberg in 1995. To qualify for the Dogma "seal of approval" a film must comply to Dogma's "vow of chastity" which includes using only available light and sound, avoiding false conventions (such as props), and eliminating all traces of directorial personality—including the director's credit. Inspired by such dreamily idealistic notions of formal restraint, British novelists Nicholas Blincoe and Matt Thorne founded the New Puritans earlier this year: their ten-point Manifesto embraces an allegedly "puritan" code of writing, defined by pledges to "shun poetry," "avoid elaborate punctuation," and (my personal favorite) "eschew flashbacks."

08. In my own experience, the common denominator uniting nearly every new business pitch I have witnessed over the past decade lies in the misguided notion that a single idea is capable of revolutionizing anything, let alone the Internet. More troubling still than this is the expectation that revolution can be achieved through, um, *software*. Though I willingly acknowledge the unparalleled global progress in interpersonal telecommunications systems (consider the advances in mobile computing, for instance) I do not accept the notion that there is one person, or advancement, or piece of software or hardware, in or out of the box, that will fundamentally alter (let alone "kill") the Internet.

09. The legacy of the clickable button is a study in misinterpretation. Buttons, when they do not slip through buttonholes as ways of fastening our clothing, are little more than miniature mechanisms for managing power: we switch them on or off, adjust their settings from low to high, push them in elevators to travel up and down. In the interests of spatial economy, buttons tend to be small, scaled to the circumference of an adult fingertip. They are not gender specific, and have few if any cultural associations beyond their generic and increasingly iconic value as emblems of point-and-click persuasion. Buttons tend to be square or elliptical, and are frequently embellished with needlessly elaborate drop-shadows and "enhanced" with rollover responsiveness so that they do really pointless things like FLASH or BLINK to let users know they have been activated. Sadly, buttons, the unfortunate product of the last ten years of digital evolution, are as ubiquitous as they are utilitarian. At their best, perhaps, they are invisible.

And yet buttons have come to represent the idealized speed—instantaneity even—with which we characterize modern life. The misnomer here lies in the fact that although modern conveniences simplify certain activities, life's essential complications endure. Consider the telephone: does speed-dial do anything to cut through the misery that is voicemail? Is button-pushing ever used to advance one's interminable wait on hold? Still, we persist in the assumption that faster is what happens when we push buttons, and that faster is better—failing to recognize, as James Glieck observes in his insightful book, (appropriately enough, titled *Faster*) that "neither technology nor efficiency can acquire more time for you, because time is not a thing you have lost … It is what you live in."

10. Last year, the U.S. Congress passed the Commercial Space Act, legalizing the privatization of manned space flight. The same dream of wide open spaces that sent Columbus to the New World will soon send every dot-com entrepreneur to the moon in his very own customized space shuttle. Though it may be hard to imagine that the space age may indeed be dawning, it is harder, still, to accept the reality that civilian inter-planetary travel is a buyer's market. My view: once the moon has become a tourist attraction, it is a pretty safe bet to assume that its frontier credibility will be a thing of the past.

FOOTNOTES

1. The American Heritage® Dictionary of the English Language, Third Edition. Copyright © 1996, 1992 by Houghton Mifflin Company.

2. For the complete text and signatories, plus coverage of the media response to this update of Ken Garland's original 1964 Manifesto by the same title, see www.adbusters.org/campaigns/first.

3. Equally incendiary, Karl Marx and Frederick Engels' classic 1848 Communist Manifesto vilifies capitalism and sings the plight of the working man. It also predates Breton and Marinetti by a full half-century.

4. Marinetti's impassioned prose offers a comparatively radical analysis of the plethora of bad Websites in daily evidence. He writes: "A repugnant mixture is concocted from monotonous sensations and the idiotic religious emotion of listeners buddhistically drunk with repeating for the nth time their more or less snobbish or second-hand ecstasy."

5. Given the freedom, would we dance in the streets? Or destroy them? For more on the 'zine Anti-Manifesto (Safe, Effective and Free!) see the following Website: www.zyworld.com/ 10584832.fc/anti-manifesto.htm.

Today's offerings in electronic media, long considered both a product and a reflection of the pragmatism that so aptly characterizes our post-industrial society, now seek to do more: in an effort to sustain audience loyalty, the goal today is to pierce the psychological veil separating personal and public, author and audience, time and space. This essay suggests that while the desire to reach people emotionally may appear perfectly respectable, it is the fact that emotional resonance exists at the expense of intellectual truth that is so troubling.

: Teasing the Nerves:
The Art of Technological Persuasion

Audiences love a good cry. Better yet, a really juicy disaster. This combined lure of misery and mayhem has proven, of late, to sustain TV ratings, increase box office receipts, and promote Internet usage better than the most imaginative fictions could ever hope to do. From the sordid dramas (divorce, paparazzi) that led the People's Princess to lose her life to the sexual dalliances (dishonesty, interns) that led an American President to jeopardize his job, the world is awash in the sorts of stories that feed our apparently endless thirst for tragedy, scandal, and confession—the police blotter writ large. In an age in which information and entertainment are so easily expedited to the average viewer, it comes as little surprise, perhaps, that said viewer will, in most cases, turn to the screen first.

And why? Simply stated, it is a familiar reflex: push a button and tune into something. Anything. And quite often, *nothing*—but with personalized newscasts, push technology, and satellite feeds, the up-to-the-minute capacities boasted by what we broadly characterize as "electronic" media give us the illusion that we are, at the very least, in the know. Whether we are bookmarking a URL or tuning into CNN—or even watching a film with mesmerizing special effects—such is our apparent trust in the screen as a reliable source of information delivery that we appear willing to see, hear, believe, and feel just about anything.

But can we actually be made to feel something, merely by staring at a screen? Actually, it is not a screen that we depend upon but multiple screens, and it is the simultaneous availability of multiple types of media that collectively shape, mediate, and, in many cases, distort our perceptions—visual, aural, emotional, intellectual, even physical—in a kind of senseless yet seamless swirl of televised, projected, and beamed messages. And increasingly, it seems, such intrusive (if not entirely manipulative) tactics inform a substantial amount of what we are exposed to, from all sides, on a daily basis.

Oddly, in spite of the sheer number of "interactive" media options available to us at any given moment, ours remains a passive genera-tion, indeed. And what separates contemporary cultural attitudes from those of a century ago is precisely this: the tremendous premium we place on leisure. Today, we crave maximum choice with minimum effort, growing more accustomed to receiving than transmitting, better at consuming than creating, finding ourselves increasingly reliant upon the multiple screens that collectively define and confine our daily data feeds—even if the information we receive is misleading or slanted or false. The more we grow accustomed—indeed, addicted—to the screens around us, whether in the form of television, computer, film, or a combination thereof, the more we imprison our minds and restrict our capacity to exercise thoughtful, independent judgment.

In this pessimistic, though perhaps realistic, portrayal of contemporary spectatorship, the precipice between believ-ability and brainwashing grows narrower by the second. Our critical faculties compromised—or at the very least signifi-cantly diminished—we leave ourselves prone to a degree of psychic suggestion unprecedented in this century. Indeed, today's offerings in electronic media, long considered both a product—and a reflection—of the very pragmatism that underscores our post-industrial culture, now seek to do more than merely service the demands of an impatient public. Recent efforts in television programming, game design, and even movie deals are going one step further: in an effort to secure and sustain audience loyalty, the goal now is to engage the viewer by piercing the psychological veil separating personal and public, time and space, me and you.

Sound like a harsh assessment of contemporary media? Probably. But what appears increasingly true is the striking degree to which information, education, and entertainment each employ a closely intertwined combination of design, tech-nology, and psychology to engage audiences in new and increasingly invasive ways. Beyond speed and software and special effects lie a host of sophisticated psychological methods that strive, in countless ways, to reach audiences with even more mesmerizing pull. Such methods—some highly deliberate and scientific, others more experimental and unpredictable—are proving to be increasingly seductive to viewers of all media. And in some cases, they are proving to be more destructive as well.

FLASH ATTACKS
Consider the case, in the winter of 1998, of the Japanese TV cartoon show that was linked to reports of illness among as many as 12,000 people—most of them children. The program combined two supersonic animation techniques: alternatively flashing lights (to cause a sense of tension—what the Japanese call "paka-paka") and a single, strong beam of red light (referred to in the general press as "flash"). These so-called "flash attacks" led to a virtual eruption of spontaneous seizures, particularly among very young viewers who were rushed by the thousands to local emergency rooms. It soon became clear that those afflicted had been watching the TV show in question, leading certain medical researchers to characterize the condition as a form of "optically stimulated epilepsy." Observed one: "This may be the first case of mass suffering from photo stimulation."

Within days, Japanese broadcasters agreed to draw up voluntary guidelines for programs to help shield children from such attacks: but the damage had, in a sense, been done. The idea that watching television, long considered a passive and essentially innocent activity, could result in such a calamitous medical emergency is horrifying.

Moreover, that animation techniques themselves—edited to maximum dramatic and visual effect—could be transmitted at such accelerated frequencies so as to cause literal convulsions in the viewer, raises the notion of TV as a mind-numbing activity to both new and considerably worrisome levels.

But mostly it is just scary: scary to think of those small and vulnerable children, perched in front of those seemingly harmless screens, watching a cartoon one minute and struggling to regain consciousness the next. Scary that technology can transport us so far, and so fast. Scary to think of the viewer as victim.

A PSYCHIC BORDER

But television is not the only culprit here—and such psychological manipulation is not always accidental. At Microsoft, for example, game developers eager to maximize Internet participation are researching ways of mimicking deeply personal, human responses to play: they describe it as "teasing the nerves." Microsoft's Alexey Pajtinov (who invented the bestselling computer game *Tetris*) describes a goal of creating a game with "emotional rhythm" that "transports a player across a psychic border...alternating a sense of achievement and loss, pleasure and disappointment." Such efforts may seem irrelevant, indulgent, or even immaterial...then again, the multi-billion dollar computer and video game market is anything but immaterial. (Some analysts estimate that its future lies predominantly online, and predict that by the year 2005 the industry itself will expand to 20$ billion.)

By all indications, the shoot-em-up action games that dominated the video market a decade ago appear to be on the wane, giving way to games of increased intellectual skill, spatial subtlety, and narrative complexity. Using the Internet as an international playing field, these new games find themselves in an excellent position to transport themselves across multiple borders: recreational, geographic, and, yes, perhaps even psychic. It is worth noting, too, that such goals are not reserved for game design alone: over in software development, Micosoft's suite of integrated office products—including Windows, Office and BackOffice—was initially being marketed in an advertising campaign under the rubric "Digital Nervous System," followed by the ominous tagline: "It's how information becomes intelligence."

OUTWITTING THE INTELLECT

Like "smart" used to suggest intuitive ability (think "smart" machines), the notion of "intelligence" as an artificially simulated behavior suggests the opportunity to alter the mind. But does it offer license to alter the facts as well? Suddenly, it seems, intellectual capabilities are being seen as something malleable—commodities to be packaged and sold, manipulated, and even bypassed entirely in this all-out effort to zap the audience. Like a giant, panoramic stun gun, the opportunities for encouraging viewers to suspend judgment in favor of an immediate emotional response are perhaps most amplified on the big screen. The idea, for example, that 1,500 people losing their lives in the frigid temperatures of the North Atlantic should immediately bring to mind a love triangle raises questions about what today's audiences are looking for. Or, perhaps more importantly, what they are willing to forget.

Certainly, the opportunity to dramatize the greatest disaster of the twentieth century is itself an enormous temptation for anyone besieged by nostalgia ... and banking on a crowd-pleaser. Add to this the chance to recreate the aristocratic splendors of 1912 (colorful costumes and plummage) as well as the grim realities of those less fortunate (monochromatic costumes and steerage) plus the underwater footage and The Big Crash itself and *Titanic* was a blockbuster movie waiting to happen. Despite cost overruns and extensive delays, the film opened to overwhelming praise: as of this writing, it is the third highest-grossing movie in history. Director James Cameron received only the most prestigious award nominations, the highest commendations, and the most gushing reviews in the popular press. "At the close of the century," wrote one prominent New York film critic, "Cameron is pushing at cinema much as D. W. Griffith did at the start, raising the stakes of the spectacular, outwitting the intellect, and heading straight for the guts."

Clearly, the desire to reach people emotionally is, in and of itself, a perfectly respectable goal. It is the idea however, that emotional resonance exists at the expense of intellectual truth that is so troubling. Underscoring this fundamental desire, too, lies the initial goal of determining what defines an audience: such demographic inquiry has long been the domain of market researchers, their data fueled by focus group findings, and fed, particularly in the United States, by an almost evangelical devotion to public opinion polls. Can the power of personalized technology combine with the reach of networked media to ease the spirit and stroke the soul? No doubt the engineers at Microsoft are working on this right now. Progress notwithstanding, there must be better ways to make an audience cry.

When he introduced his theory of relativity in 1905, Einstein revolutionized 500 years of quantum physics by challenging a fundamentally logical supposition. Looking back, what was particularly striking was the aesthetic response that paralleled his thinking over the next quarter of a century: from cubist fragmentation, to surrealist displacement, to futurist provocation, to constructivist juxtaposition—each, in a sense, a radical reconsideration of spatial paradigms in a material world. This essay critiques the scarcity of sustained innovation in today's media, and identifies three ideological components—personal displacement, physical dematerialization, and spatial demarcation—that collectively define a new model for thinking about space beyond the mere flatness of the screen.

From the fifteenth through the early twentieth centuries, our understanding of space and time was bound by an unflinching belief in the four cornerstones of physical reality, framed by what is routinely considered to be a kind of Newtonian paradigm: space, time, energy and mass. Like Euclidean space, which defines directional thinking in vectors (top, bottom, left, and right), the western concept of space was absolute: boundless and infinite, flat and inert, knowable and fixed.

Then in 1905, Albert Einstein revolutionized 500 years of quantum physics by suggesting that energy and mass are interchangeable, and that space and time share a kind of uninterrupted continuum—proving, quite simply, that the only true constant is the speed of light.

Today, as we sit illuminated by the glare of a billion computer screens, we are living proof that he was right. The computer is our connection to the world. It is an information source, an entertainment device, a communications portal, a production tool. We design on it and for it, and are its most loyal subjects, its most agreeable audience. But we are also its prisoners: trapped in a medium in which visual expression must filter through a protocol of uncompromising programming scripts, "design" must submit to a series of commands and regulations as rigorous as those that once defined Swiss typography. Aesthetic innovation, if indeed it exists at all, occurs within ridiculously preordained parameters: a new plug-in, a modified code, the capacity to make pictures and words "flash" with a mouse in a nonsensical little dance. We are all little filmmakers, directing on a pathetically small screen—yet broadcasting to a potentially infinite audience. This in itself is conflicting (not to mention corrupting) but more important, what are we making? What are we inventing? What are we saying that has not been said before?

Where is the avant-garde in new media?

What Einstein did was challenge a fundamentally logical supposition. And looking back, what was particularly striking was the aesthetic response that paralleled his thinking over the next quarter of a century: from cubist fragmentation, to surrealist displacement, to futurist provocation, to constructivist juxtaposition—each, in a sense, a radically new reconsideration of spatial paradigms in a material world. And while there was dissent, there was also consensus: streamlined shapes, a rejection of ornament, an appeal to minimalism, to functionalism, to simplicity. A response to the machine age—not just to the machine.

It is, of course, a particular conceit of post-modernism that a lack of consensus is precisely what separates the second half of the twentieth century from the first. But does this alone explain the creative disparity so evident in electronic space? More likely, it is not space that demands our attention now so much as our *representation* of space, and our ability to mould and manage ideas within boundaries that are fundamentally intangible: what we need is a reconsideration of spatial paradigms in an immaterial world.

To date, our efforts to define space on the Internet have required a basic fluency in the fundamental markup languages that are needed to bring design to life; SGML, HTML, XML, WAP protocols, and soon, with the imminent convergence of television and the Web, TVML. Each deals in linear, logical, Cartesian alignments: ones and zeroes, x's and y's, pull-down menus and scrolling screens. Supporting software products remain essentially rooted in the finite world of printed matter: most are based on editing and publishing models and, not surprisingly, have a page-oriented display system, adding additional "media" as needed to extend or evoke information beyond the customary offerings of text and image. And though they purport to be more multidimensional in nature, architectural opportunities to place 3D models in "space" offer little more than sculptural simulations, providing basic toolsets for rotating geometric forms which mimic movement in a primitive, awkward, cartoony sort of way.

Nowhere do we see the kind of variety, or depth, or topographical distinctions we might expect given the boundless horizons of Internet space. Nowhere do we see a new spatial paradigm, an alternative way of representing ideas—of experimenting, for example, with what philosopher Gaston Bachelard lyrically refers to as "the psychological elasticity of an image." Nowhere do we see, or feel, or discover a new sense of place, freed of the shackles of Cartesian logic—space that might ebb and flow, expand and contract, dimensional space, elliptical space, new and unusual space. Homepages, indeed! What could possibly be said to be homey about the Web—or even about TV, for that matter? Do we find shelter, permanence, or comfort there? Does it smell good? Is it warm, familiar, personal? What domestic truths are mirrored in the space of the screen, projected back to us, and beamed elsewhere?

This is one of the more irritating myths about the electronic age, yet one that perpetually seems to reinstate itself with each new technological advance. Space on the screen is just that: on the screen. Not in it. Not of it. Design tools are mere control mechanisms perpetuating the illusion that Internet space is made up of pages, of words, of flat screens. Why is it that design thinking remains so brainwashed by this notion? The world of the Internet is its own peculiar galaxy, with its own constellations of information, its own orbits of content. And it is by no means flat.

DISPLACEMENT (OF THE OBSERVER)

The rectangle of the computer monitor frames everything we see on screen. Our peripheral vision is at all times influenced—if not altogether compromised—by the stultifying presence of the container, an unforgiving geometry if there ever was one. (Oddly, this same frame circumscribes the photographer looking through the camera lens— yet here, the frame itself fades from view the minute the shutter clicks. Not so when the mouse clicks, however.) More puzzling still, the lure of networked interaction on the Web is predicated on precisely the opposite set of conditions: though circumscribed by a steadfast box, virtual space celebrates the intangible gesture, the dematerialized transaction, the inconquerable, timeless exchange.

What has not been recognized is the extent to which the viewer is a moving target. Are our conceptions of electronic space lodged in geometric exactitude in an effort to harness the dynamic of an unruly audience?

Efforts to break out of the box—and here some of the experimental studies conducted at places like the MIT Media Lab, among other schools and research facilities, merit attention—have addressed this conflict by creating what might broadly be characterized as "ambient" media: Websites projected on walls, push-button and hand-held devices replaced by portable, mutable media that gesture and respond to sensory input—all are attempts both to reinterpret and reinforce monitor-free interaction between human beings and the machines that serve them.

But this trend in portability points to a broader, more significant cultural phenomenon: in an age in which perception itself is synonymous with transience, we remain more preoccupied with the space *surrounding* the technology than with the space *inside* the technology.

Though this is particularly true of the Internet, our understanding of television space is not dissimilar. Here, too, we chart the course, control the path, and click our way through a kind of visual no-man's land. What has not been examined is the degree to which our spatial perception skews, like a reflex, as if to automatically compensate for the fragmented nature of the journey.

DEMATERIALIZATION (OF WHAT IS BEING OBSERVED)
What is missing from Internet space is not only a defining set of physical boundaries but the temporal references that give implicit direction—meaning, even—to our actions. Not so in the 24x7 space of the Internet, where space and time do, in fact, share an uninterrupted continuum, and where the conventions of timekeeping—clocks, calendars, the occasional sunrise—are rendered virtually immaterial. (The television tactic of rationalizing time through programming will itself be rendered somewhat immaterial as well if the promises of WebTV are fulfilled. The introduction of TiVo—"TV your way,"—is the first significant step in this direction.) More interesting, perhaps, is the shape of things as they are happening: indeed, the qualitative difference between hyperspace and more passive screen environments (television and film, for example) lies in the celebration of the journey itself. In interactive environments, the promenade—and its implicit digressions—are as important as the destination.

This is as close to a definition of "vernacular" as we are likely to get in electronic space: if the viewer moves through the information, and the information itself is moving, it is this kinetic activity—this act of moving—that circumscribes our perception, dominates our senses, and becomes, in a very noticeable sense, the new prevailing aesthetic.

DEMARCATION (OF NEW BOUNDARIES):

It is easy to equate the notion of wide, open spaces with freedom and opportunity—qualities that we associate with the bold ambitions of early settlers, of westward expansion and manifest destiny and the inimitable American frontier. Such pioneering spirit has long retained its almost mythic status in modern culture, symbolizing freedom, individualism, and a kind of peculiarly American democracy.

Like the once-open West, Internet space is uncharted territory. Air is free and land is cheap. And, indeed, its presence in our lives points to a kind of utopian idealism prefigured a century ago, when we thrilled to the notion of pure, mechanized efficiency.

But today, the boundaries have shifted. New boundaries are enabled by new kinds of technologies, by the demands of new products and the imperatives of new economies. The Internet is all these: a kind of chameleon-like civilization that seems to perpetually remap its identity in response to the ever-changing demands of a mercurial market. In a world in which everything is customized, even our boundaries are on the move.

So it all fits together: portable media, transient journeys, movable boundaries. Unlike our nineteenth-century predecessors, we have not shaped this new world with nuance and detail, with an urban-industrial east or a preservationist west. We have not responded with a hue and cry borne of the kind of revolutionary fervor typified by early twentieth-century designers and artists. More likely, our response has been a reactive one: to technological imperatives, to pragmatic considerations, and to each other. To think beyond these practicalities is to respond to a broader and more compelling challenge: the idea that, as designers, we might begin to tackle the enormous opportunities to be had in staking claim to and shaping a new and unprecedented universe. There, if anywhere, lies the new avant-garde.

Minimize difference. Maximize reproducibility. Make it easy, accessible, understandable to all. This is the univernacular, ultra-homogenized and distinction-free, the international language of the status-quo. Indeed, as the boundary between public and private dissolves further into the untamed wilderness of our modern sensibilities, the degree to which design can be used to articulate any distinctions remains highly questionable. This essay explores the perilous line between privacy and publicity, examining the increasing reliance upon representational thinking and the yearning for mass appeal that continue to dominate our visual expectations in the digital realm.

"The most characteristic quality of modern man lies in the remarkable antithesis between an interior which fails to correspond to any exterior and an exterior which fails to correspond to any interior."
—FREDERICK NIETZSCHE
The Uses and Abuses of History, 1874

"I am at two with nature."
—WOODY ALLEN

I am standing in my kitchen preparing dinner for my children when the promotional copy on a package of Perdue Chicken grabs my attention. It seems Perdue is launching a national search (seeking a "poultry Picasso") to redesign the classic nugget. "Your Child Could Win You A Trip to Paris!" it reads. "The shape they draw today could become the chicken nugget they eat tomorrow." Now I am really hooked. I turn to the fine print. "Entries will be judged by an independent panel of judges on the following criteria:
1. Originality.
2. Creativity.
3. Ease of reproducability of nugget design."

The degree to which "ease of reproducability of nugget design" so perfectly characterizes the present state of design in networked environments strikes me like a bolt of lightning. And while I would like to report that my thoughts, upon this realization, drifted to Martin Heidegger or Giles Deleuze, to existentialism or metaphysics or even postmodernism, alas, they did not. I did, however, briefly delight in the presumption that this domestic revelation likened me to a kind of latter-day Proust, waxing poetic over freshly-baked madeleines—but in truth, I cannot lay claim to any such poeticism, either in the form of sensory awareness or sentient nostalgia. The chicken was, after all, still sitting there in the package, waiting for me to transform it into something, well, *edible.*

Consider the following: you are being asked to create a Website, to take abstract data and transform it into something, well, designed. You are told "the user" (read "human") wants it clean and clear, uncomplicated and accessible. When you "drill down" (read "read") to the fifteen hundredth screen, it should retain its consistent "look and feel" (read "design"). Easy access! Consistent navigation! Sound functionality!

Oh—and by the way, when it bakes up in the oven, you need to still recognize its essential shape.

Minimize difference. Maximize reproducibility. Make it easy, accessible, understandable to all. This is the univernacular: ultra-homogenized and distinction-free, the international language of the status-quo. Indeed, as the boundary between public and private dissolves further into the untamed wilderness of our modern sensibilities, the degree to which design can be used to articulate *any* distinctions remains highly questionable. Identity—whether it is understood to be private, as in the identity of an individual, or public, as in the identity of a place—is riddled with ambiguity. Stripped of the physical references that define self and site, gender and geography, we drift in a peaceful (if monotonous) no-man's land of intangible relationships and dematerialized transactions. Screen names masquerade as real names. Jargon replaces language. Hieroglyphs and buttons proliferate. We locate one another through a mysterious wayfinding system of numbers and letters, keywords and bookmarks, abbreviations and acronyms, random punctuation slicing and dicing through run-on sentences. It is a loopy lexicon of dot-this and slash-that and e-everything else, that is about as qualitatively informative about the "places" you are visiting as a pre-fab suburban development.

So we click. Scroll up. Page down. Life on the screen becomes a rigorous, Cartesian journey from east to west, up north, down south. It is an aesthetically simplistic, curatorially ill-defined flip book, in which four-dimensional experience is forcibly retrofitted to conform to the unforgiving parameters of two-dimensional representation. "Life" in this new "public" realm is physically constrained and programmatically curtailed by the economics of space (via screen) and time (via bandwidth) and, increasingly, appears largely predisposed to adopt the broadly accepted cultural bias opposing idiosyncrasy or individuality or anything that dares challenge the essential rules of the system itself. Fast and easy and mass-produced—this is the "space" we inhabit, the "landscape" we peruse, the "environment" we, as designers, are helping to build.

And we are cowards, because we are doing so little to change it, to question its lack of innovation, to challenge the ludicrous banality that characterizes its essential mass appeal. Instead, we hide behind creatively engineered pedigrees—calling ourselves "strategists" and "consultants" and, God help me, "information architects," when we are really just graphic designers. And despite being graphic designers—despite being in the business of two-dimensional representation—we continue to talk-the-univernacular-talk while we perpetuate the hackneyed assumptions and pretentious misconceptions that do so much to frame this culture, yet do so little to advance our profession. I know I am asking for trouble here, but how else to interpret the 1999 American Center for Design conference entitled *No Where, Now Here?* (While I applaud the conference's alleged focus on ubiquitous computing, the degree to which this title seemed to glorify ambiguity just sent me reeling.) How can it be that the complex, pluralistic cultural influences that bring shape and meaning to life in the real world have no symbolic meaning, inferred topology or ideological parallel in virtual space? How could we have come this far and still be—*no where?*

If indeed we are "no where," it is likely a consequence of the prevailing character of the electronic landscape which, if understood as a "public" space, is essentially uncharted territory—wide open, amorphous, and free. It is also unlimited real estate, and, perhaps for this reason, presents itself as quintessentially democratic. And yet it is really quite the opposite: this new "Virtual Republic" is limited by some very real practical constraints, constraints that have little to do with people, but have a lot to do with machines. Efficient maybe, but far from democratic.

Nevertheless, what remains certain is the fact that the boundaries between public life and private circumstances continue to shift. And increasingly, electronic space—sometimes called the electronic frontier (which always lends a kind of faux-theatrical, swashbuckling tone of heroism to it all)—is all attitude. It is all packaging. It is all virtual. It is a compendium of micro-controlled and highly regulated two-dimensional amalgamations of flattened information masquerading as "spaces"and "places," but let's be honest: they are not spaces. They are screens. What we think about, and shape, and design are the façades for spaces: they attempt, however crudely, to simulate doors and walls and windows, to mimic a texture, to flag a path. But the architectural metaphor, though applicable to a point, is both misunderstood and deeply flawed. How does what we design represent the dynamic journey, the relevant context, the momentarily fixed visual snapshot of time and space that Walter Benjamin would likely have characterized as a "fleeting reflection"?

Why, too, do we talk about navigation but never about circulation, about secure transactions but never about shelter, about pageviews but never about program, or passage, or promenade? Probably because at some very basic level we recognize that the design and planning of virtual spaces does not, in reality, mirror the cultural and temporal conditions of the built environment. If anything, its appeal lies in the utopian conceit of its otherness. The Virtual Republic is the land of critical mass. It is unmenacing and ghetto-free. There is no urban decay here, no civic strife, and—hackers notwithstanding—little we would characterize, in human terms, as crime.

Then again, there is no natural light here, either. Or air. There are no seasons, nor are there any apparent visual cues denoting the physical passage of time: it is all collapsed into one single 24x7 acceleration capsule. And while I am not necessarily advocating that we replicate such real-world qualities here, I would argue that it is this, the physical, gestural, even emotionally processed nuances—what makes Prague different from Paris from Peoria, let's say—that are absent in an environment that is by definition circumscribed by code-based, protocol-driven, monitor-enframed, two-dimensional representational thinking.

This emphasis on representational thinking lies at the core of the univernacular. (And arguably, of graphic design.) In digital environments, it is what frames our daily odysseys, our meandering click-throughs, our digital peregrinations which are tracked by software that monitors our every move. Funny: we reserve the right to be private only when our transactions are protected—behind firewalls, behind secure servers—proving, as architectural theorist Beatriz

Colomina has suggested, that "privacy is what exceeds the eyes." If you cannot see it, it must be private. And if private, it must be personal. And if personal, it cannot be mass-produced, so maybe—just maybe—it can be, well, *designed*.

But it is not. And while we might define real privacy in material terms—we can close a door, and even lock it—is there anything left in the electronic sphere that truly exceeds the eyes? Here in Six-Degrees-of-Separationville, is there anything sacred, devoid of public scrutiny, freed from the shackles of surreptitious media surveillance? Today's great technological euphemism for privacy is customization: its philosophical premise lies in the notion that technology can be responsive to an individual's tastes and needs, its insatiable appetite for retail therapy. Customization may be personal, but it is also propaganda: it makes "you" the brand! Indeed, the sudden ubiquity of the prefix "my" on Websites around the globe—*MyYahoo, MyEbay, MyNavelGazingWebCam*—offers startling proof that mass production has reached such an all-time high that even absolute possessives have become generic branding devices. Observes critic and cultural theorist Dave Hickey: "In an increasingly diffuse and complex post-industrial world, we cling to the last vestige of industrial thinking: the presumption of mass-produced identity and ready-made experience—a presumption that makes the expression, appreciation, or even the perception of our everyday distinctions next to impossible."

So distinctions are passé. Conformity rocks. As we all hold hands and sing another refrain of "We Are the World" how nice that we can sleep soundly knowing there is a place for everything, and everything is in its place. It is so easy. After all, everything "looks and feels" so much like everything else! We rejoice in the promises of a new economy that eliminates the middleman and promotes equality among the rest of us. Somewhere along the way, we all drank from the same spiked Kool Aid. There is clearly strength—if not apathy—in numbers.

Meanwhile, the univernacular rules. I said I would not discuss Heidegger, but I lied: his critique of modern technology hinges on a process he calls "enframing" which he explains as the reduction of matter to quantifiable, measurable, and predictable terms. Mass-produced, ready-made, and easy. Kind of like the univernacular.

And, indeed, rather like chicken nuggets, too.

The simplicity that characterizes de Stijl thinking—and the order that can be traced in Dutch painting as far back as the seventeenth century—suggest conceptually provocative yet surprisingly practical methods for organizing space and for achieving visually engaging solutions in screen-based media. Such a hypothesis suggests that we reconsider the screen as a kind of picture plane: with this in mind, this essay suggests that to challenge the picture plane is to radically adjust our thinking about what a screen is, what a computer is, and what role design plays in the mix.

: De Stijl, New Media, and the Lessons of Geometry

In his collected essays, *Architecture and Disjunction,* Bernard Tschumi argues that frames as architectural elements derive their meaning through juxtaposition. "They establish memory," he writes, "of the preceding frame, of the course of events." This idea that a structural element can serve a graphically direct yet intensely personal need is a compelling notion indeed, and recalls the ambitions of earlier twentieth-century visionaries who sought to embrace social order and spiritual harmony through simple, formal means: this is perhaps most true of the de Stijl group, an informal confederation of artists, architects, and designers working in Holland between 1917 and 1931. Strangely, however, while the lessons of modernism in general—and de Stijl in particular—have found their way into contemporary design education and practice, the invaluable formal principles upon which this thinking was based remain virtually absent in the design of new media.

In 1915 and 1916, theosophist M. H. J. Schoenmaekers published "The New Image of the World" and "Principles of Plastic Mathematics." Suggesting that reality might best be expressed as a series of opposing forces—a formal polarity of horizontal and vertical axes and a juxtaposition of primary colors—the author posited a new image of the world, expressed with "a controllable precision, a conscious penetration of reality and exact beauty." In an age in which we are bombarded with frequent, dense, and often contradictory messages about what it is we are saying, meaning, and making, this statement is refreshingly straightforward. Read literally, it also provides an inspirational way of deconstructing the complex role design plays in our increasingly digital culture. Most important, perhaps, to the designer lamenting the intractable restrictions of today's technological climate, the formal language of de Stijl—and its celebration of the purity of the x/y axis—is inspiration indeed.

As the primary theoretical influence behind the de Stijl movement, Schoenmaekers' thinking paralleled the evolution of a reductive visual vocabulary that embraced ideals at once utilitarian and utopian: with this vocabulary, artists such as Piet Mondrian and Theo van Doesberg produced work that, in its spare elegance, has had a lasting effect on twentieth-century aesthetics. Thought to be radical at the time of their initial publication, today these ideas are surprisingly relevant, as they—and the work they influenced—suggest a deceptively simple way to think about the formal, temporal, and cultural phenomena that collectively define new media. In an effort to resolve the relationships between structural form and transient content, between cyclical time and infinite space, and between a message transmitted and a message received, the propositions of de Stijl suggest an ideal paradigm with which to evaluate the role and effectiveness of design in an electronic age.

To practitioners of de Stijl, the reduction of pure form was considered a symbolic translation of complex cultural ideals. While it possessed no notable political cause *per se*—unlike Malevich and the Russian constructivists, or Marinetti and the Italian futurists—it argued for a kind of convergent thinking that links it unequivocally to the culture of new media. The goals of elevating society, of bridging the gap between the collective and the individual, and of gesturing to a kind of utopian ideal were expressed enthusiastically in the work, as well as in the writing of position papers, exhibition catalogs, commercial publications, and other forms of propaganda. These manifestoes are evocative reminders of de Stijl ideology: in their evangelism and rhetoric, they bear a strong resemblance to much of the propaganda espoused by contemporary new media culture. Unlike contemporary media, however, the visual evidence of de Stijl thinking was both surprisingly simple and enormously sophisticated. Perhaps for this reason, it was also quite beautiful. In the wake of such triumphant breakthroughs in the distillation of human thought, why have we veered so far from the lessons of modernism?

Today, as designers struggle to define better ways of representing ideas in two-, three-, and four-dimensional space, Schoenmaekers' ideas, dating from more than a century ago, offer us a way to better understand and clarify these questions. To begin with, the question of "controllable precision" suggests a standard for designers struggling to rationalize their role in the convergent morass of telecommunications commonly known as "new media." Here, the very value of design is in question: as interpersonal exchanges coexist and multiply in a landscape laden with sophisticated electronic options, one might argue that the function of design is marginalized—if not rendered entirely obsolete—or that the role of the designer itself is imperiled. We have perhaps unwittingly ceded control: to our computers, to our audience, to the demands of a new and increasingly global economy. But the opportunity to define—even celebrate—precision lies at the heart of what we can and should do. This elevates and objectifies our role, and redefines our mission as architects of a new visual order.

"Controllable precision" is of course impossible in an environment characterized by such random and perpetual change. What is possible, however, is to think about design as a system of limitations, and to consider the role of the designer as one who articulates that system. Establishing a grid, understanding the permutations of a template as a flexible armature within which information can be delivered, is a good example of the graphical application of such a system, in print as well as on the screen. With the ongoing advances in browser technologies (such as frames, borderless frames, tables, and so forth) a more resolved formal articulation of space is now possible on the screen, making "controllable precision" an eminently achievable goal.

This system—the establishment of the template, its formal attributes, and its compositional potential for iterative recombination—is not only the principal function of design in online media, but its greatest contribution. Conversely, what happens between the frames is not: the indulgent, memory-intensive aesthetic that evidences itself on many proprietary Websites only serves to demonstrate how technical complexity short-circuits "good" design. With error prompts pre-empting any opportunity for theatrical or visual impact, the mood is irrevocably broken, an enduring reminder that a shield of intrusive technology lies between you and your screen. This is the "interface" at its worst: simply stated, this is what happens when design gets in the way.

Alternatively, the simplicity that characterizes de Stijl thinking—and the order that can be traced in Dutch painting as far back as the seventeenth century—suggest a better model for organizing space and achieving visually engaging and functionally successful solutions. In his own work, van Doesberg identified this purist reduction as an attempt to "expel the narrative." In this view, the designer is the director rather than the actor, and design is less about experience, and more about framing the experience. The success of this proposition rests largely in rethinking ways of articulating space, and suggests that we reconsider the screen as a kind of picture plane. To challenge the picture plane is to radically adjust our thinking about what a screen is, what a computer is, and what role design plays in the mix. Central to this is a formal appreciation of modernism and a fundamental understanding of its *lingua franca:* geometry.

This appeal to modernism, however, has been virtually overlooked in these early days of new media design. Today, the prevailing aesthetic leans away from realism, opting instead for a primitive sampling of poorly rendered, often cartoon-like illustrations masquerading as familiar, habitable spaces. Worse still, with the advent of Virtual Reality Modeling Language (VRML) what was objectionable in 2D now becomes horrifying in 3- and 4D. Here, Schoenmaekers' notion of "penetrating reality" suggests an intriguing alternative to such tiresome examples of forced and phony simulacra. The opportunity to reconstruct reality rejects the overused models and metaphors that currently exist—the faux street scene, the mock desktop—in favor of a simplified and inherently more flexible visual vocabulary—one based on simple geometric form.

The suggestion that geometry can address the human condition lies at the core of classic architectural discourse, and is everywhere present in the ideology and practice of de Stijl. Described as "neoplastic," architecture in this period favored a kind of elementary constructivism evidenced in anti-decorative, asymmetrical, and colorful explorations of spatial displacement. Such experiments—the famous red, blue, and yellow Rietveldt chair (1918), for example—indicated the extent to which simple form could explode with new and provocative possibility. Mondrian's *Broadway Boogie Woogie* (1926) was an attempt to codify the dynamic pulse of the city through the restrained use of horizontal and vertical lines, the expression of two opposing forces. It is no coincidence that this work gestured to the space beyond the limits of the canvas: indeed, the desire to embrace infinite space was in no small way influenced by Einstein's theory of relativity, which had been published several years earlier.

Like the de Stijl artists, we can identify with the imposed recti-
linear parameters circumscribing our work, as we struggle to define
the opportunities for creative expression on screen. We can share their
pointed fascination with infinite space as we explore the limitless real
estate options introduced by the phenomenon of cyberspace. But
unlike them, our work today has yet to reveal itself as inspired,
informed by their legacy, their thinking, the empirical evidence of
their prolific labors. In the end, as reality itself is called into question
by the notion of virtual space and the users (read audiences) who
dwell there, "beauty" (not to mention "exact beauty") is indeed in the
eye of the beholder. This is of course the true goal of interactivity:
designers often struggle in particular with the intangible temporal
component implicit in these new media, where experience is meant
to be customized and mutable. How can design address consistency—
of place, of identity, of need—and still speak to the perpetual changes
that characterize the transient nature of these phenomena? Of great
relevance to new media, de Stijl practitioners concerned themselves
with resolving the relationship between the static and the dynamic.
Their interest in challenging the formal interplay of geometric
elements suggests that the orchestration of components can simulta-
neously gesture to the fixed and to the flexible, to the precision as well
as to the ellusiveness of "exact beauty." In this view, the same reductive visual vocabulary cannot only support such seemingly conflicting
ideals (static/kinetic, variable/constant, universal/unique) but can
perhaps begin to suggest more innovative solutions for structuring
new systems, mapping new spaces, and reaching new audiences
along the way.

For the surrealists, montage represented a way to rethink not only form and its relationship to content, but an opportunity to rethink art in a changing social context, and to capture the complexity of varied human experience on a single surface. Their preoccupation with immediacy itself presages the speed which we typically expect from contemporary media offerings. To rethink surrealist ideology in a contemporary context, what was desireable on canvas has now become eminently achievable on screen. This is sensory montage: a merging of disparate phenomena and kinetic media that collectively bespeak the complexity of our modern, and increasingly fragmented, human condition.

: Sensory Montage:
Rethinking Fusion and Fragmentation

Recent reports on the miraculous successes of animal cloning have prompted reactions ranging from outrage to optimism, at once renewing our fear and our faith in man's capacity to triumph over the physical limits of nature. Here, we are without question witnessing one of the most remarkable feats of modern science and, not surprisingly, the mind reels: with human cloning just around the corner, we find ourselves ill-equipped to comprehend the complex moral implications of such unprecedented biological hanky-panky. Conceptually, the very notion summons our darkest fantasies: exaggerated, caricature-like, borne of the kind of science fiction that typically carries with it the threat of imminent annihilation. Yet formally, cloning is an intriguing—if mysterious—notion, appealing both to our appetite for technological novelty and to our ambitions for human efficiency. In this view, perhaps, it is the user interface at its most terrifying: part man, part machine, a calculated orchestration of curated chromosomes: the ultimate design object.

But more than this, cloning is the *command-D* of modern science: will duplicating ourselves make us happier, or more productive, or more powerful because there will be two (or more) of us? A longer view suggests that cloning might easily be imagined as a kind of sophisticated tool for time-management, or a way to address what Sherry Turkle calls the "divided" self—a condition we may rightly attribute to the prevailing tone of modern life and its relentless emphasis on multitasking. (The standard Mac/Windows interface is a typical model supporting such schisms by providing multiple windows, or folders within a single surface, or screen. In Turkle's view, your identity on the computer is the sum of your distributed presence in these environments.)

As technology itself continues to inform our behaviors beyond the environment of the interface, efforts to embrace such multiplicity give way to a radically new way of thinking about the merged and multiple media that reside within the broadly defined "boundaries" of the screen. Once simple display devices, screens have become popular mechanisms for accelerated commerce, whether in the form of electronic banking, email, or televised news coverage. And while much has been written in the design press on deconstruction as a diagnostic tool for unravelling the sorts of complexities that so broadly typify these contemporary cultural phenomena, it is arguably the opposite that is true: today, the integrated sophistication of multiple media has enabled the emergence of a new vernacular, a kind of sensory montage both projected on and reflective of Turkle's notion of the divided self, the digital doppelgänger that has come to symbolize the fragmented character of contemporary culture.

In the book *Collage City,* architectural theorist Colin Rowe identifies collage as a paradigm for understanding both social fragmentation and spatial collapse. "Societies and persons assemble themselves according to their own interpretations of absolute reference and traditional value," he writes. "To a point, collage accomodates both hybrid display and the requirements of self-determination." To take Rowe at his word today—thirty years later and outside the architectural discourse within which these comments were intended to be understood—is to broadly characterize the idea of collage (or, by conjecture here, montage) as a kind of catch-all metaphor for our overly technologized lives. At the same time, it brings to mind the utopian ideals of earlier art movements whose advocates wrestled with ways of expressing the polarities dividing the individual and society, the machine and the body, nature and technology.

This thinking might be said to have its formal antecedents in cubism, where fracturing the picture plane introduced a modern alternative to representational art in favor of a more abstract idiom. In time, cubism broke down further to allow for the development of both surrealism and constructivism. It is difficult to divorce either of these movements from the political imperatives that led to their birth and eventual demise—and while we may still long for world peace, those of us dwelling among civilized nations would be hard put to condemn our respective governments of the fascism and control that characterized the creative European climate during the turbulent early years of last century. Still, looking critically at contemporary media—and here I am referring to screen-based media, including television and computer interfaces—we are arguably closer to the influences of the surrealists (and even more to their successors, the situationists, who lingered on—primarily in France—until the early 1970s) than to the geometric, and somewhat more restrictive logical order of the constructivists.

For the surrealists, montage represented a way to rethink not only form and its relationship to content, but through the unexpected juxtaposition of visual material, a way to reconsider art in a changing social context, and to capture the complexity of experience on a single surface. The surrealists' preoccupation with immediacy itself presages the speed which we typically expect from today's media offerings. Conceptually, the experience of an average day of television programming—where illogical sequences reflect targeted appeals to decidedly different audiences, virtually precluding a singular or fluid viewing experience—parallels the visual indifference evident in the "ready-made" experimental installations designed over half a century ago by Marcel Duchamp. Verbally, the rhetorical sloppiness that characterizes most email exchanges recalls the automatic, trance-like writing style of early surrealist texts drafted by André Breton and Phillipe Soupault. And visually, the merging of surfaces—and media—on contemporary multimedia screens is itself reminiscent of the surrealists' ambition to attain greater authenticity through the fusion of all the arts. (It is largely for this reason that the surrealists were drawn to the medium of film, which they saw as a way to collapse time and space, thereby probing new areas of experience.) Simply put, to rethink surrealist ideology in a contemporary context, what was desirable on canvas has now become eminently achievable on screen: a merging of disparate phenomena and kinetic media that collectively bespeak the complexity of the modern, and increasingly fragmented, human condition. In other words, sensory montage.

What is a screen? "While the noun screen connotes an outer, visible layer, the verb to screen means "to hide," notes the writer Alice Fulton. "Yet to screen a movie is to show it," she observes, "rather than obscure it." These dual definitions, or incarnations of the same word suggest the degree to which the screen itself posesses a complex and variable presence in our daily lives: as a window, linking public space and private space; as an interface, providing closure and exposure; as a mirror, reinforcing the self and enabling reciprocity across electronically linked phone lines. Screens have become our home away from home: portable and ubiquitous, they not only permit uncertainty, they revel in it. Here, we sacrifice simplicity to the lure of selection: the result is what is commonly referred to in interactive media as "option paralysis." So we channel chase on TV (and surf the Web), and the plethora of options in each medium only serves to exaggerate these nomadic, episodic journeys, where experience is by definition unpredictable.

The question of designing "experience" is frequently debated in design circles, and particularly in educational circles where students have a tendency to mistake software as a way to transform themselves miraculously into film directors. The prevailing sentiment seems influenced not only by the stylistic urge to layer, but also by the expectation that design must address new and complex audiences in new and complex ways. Layering and fragmentation are indeed ways to address complexity and change: occasionally they serve to illuminate true experience, as in the case of the Emmy award-winning broadcast title sequence to the hospital drama "E.R.," designed by Pittard Sullivan. Here the objective is to visually express the percussive pace of a major city hospital's emergency ward. But used for stylistic impact—rather than dramatic effect—it is also a way to avoid making a decision, committing to an idea, addressing an audience with focus: an example here might be *The New York Times* "Expect the World" advertising campaign, which uses blurred typography and nostalgic imagery to suggest what is, in fact, the precision of a reporting style that is this publication's greatest asset.

In screen-based media of all kinds there continues to be a tremendous emphasis on interruptive activity. Clearly, life often follows such patterns, leading one to suspect that this tendency is itself rooted in the familiar pulse of daily behavior, complete with interruption, contradiction, and fragmentation. Here is the digital doppelgänger at work: the artistic self looks for ways to extend these ideals in visually compelling ways (blur the type!) while the analytical self looks for diagnostically quantifiable results (who is watching?). Ratings on TV are like hits on Websites: they comment on consumption and traffic, report on the quantity rather than the quality (let alone the dramatic success) of the screen experience. Cultural critic Todd Gitlin explains it simply: "The (television ratings) numbers only sample sets tuned in, not necessarily shows watched, let alone grasped, remembered, loved, learned from, deeply anticipated, or mildly tolerated."

Television sends a falsely compelling signal to the public in general—and designers in particular—for several reasons. First, because it amputates the senses, editing out the sights and smells and ambient details of real experience to zero in on what can fit within the rectangle of the screen. Second, because it makes information seem more important by delivering it in fits and starts: consider the editing style of broadcast journalism, which provides the public with, quite literally, "sound bytes": shards of information that have become synonymous with the ways we access news.

In his excellent book *The Age of Missing Information,* Bill McKibben discusses the simulation of experience on the screen during the Persian Gulf War in the early 1990s, when fragmented snippets of brutal missile attacks were televised as a kind of protracted, you-are-there form of documentary journalism. It was one big serialized drama, and ratings soared as viewers reportedly went home at night to "watch the war." (McKibben pointedly observes the fundamental failure of such screen-based simulation, adding that reality junkies looking for a proper war fix might have been better advised to hire someone to toss a brick through their living room windows in the middle of the night.)

As technology advances and our needs grow more sophisticated, we look to the screen not merely as an instrument of information delivery, but also as a kind of stage set: here, Rowe's idea of "hybrid display" suggests that a singular form (the screen) may embrace multiple functions (or roles), embracing—indeed, celebrating—the very polarities that formerly characterized the schisms of modern culture. The appeal of speed, the lure of the dramatic, and a perpetual barrage of multiple media come together on the screen in a seductive play of sensory choreography: in this view, perhaps, it has a mesmer-izing, if not altogether therapeutic appeal. CNN recently reported on a technology developed for hospitals, in which a screen backlit by ten computer-operated lights was designed to simulate the orange glow of sunrise: its intention was to boost the spirits of terminally-ill patients who would otherwise be confined to four blank walls. In this context, through illumination, design, and placement, the screen enabled yet another role to be played, another self to be embraced.

The idea, of course, that the screen illuminates, mirrors, distorts, and, perhaps most of all, blurs the distinction between truth and fiction is not new. Indeed, not long after news of animal cloning made international headlines, the biggest mass suicide in American history claimed the lives of thirty-nine cult followers in a wealthy Southern California community. And while the strict ordinances uniting this group required a complete renunciation of so-called "earthly" pleasures, the followers of Heaven's Gate supported themselves as Website designers, a fact that led *Newsweek* to report—somewhat facetiously—that though removed from society, they had engaged in a professional activity that ironically placed them at the very heart of the information revolution.

The cult's only other apparently enduring link to civilized life lay in their television viewing habits: their library was stocked with a selection of conspiracy-theory videos featuring both the Branch Davidians and the U.S. Internal Revenue Service. In addition, they were faithful followers of *Star Wars*, "Star Trek" and "The X-Files." By dramatic, though somewhat macabre extension, their last farewell was made manifest in a self-eulogizing videotape in which one follower cited a debt to television, proclaiming solemnly that the time had come to "put into practice what they had learned."

It is enormously difficult to imagine what might have led thirty-nine people to willingly take their own lives, though perhaps even more difficult to imagine that their rationale took its cue from an exaggerated reading and misappropriation of biblical, astronomical, and fictional references. The model of the screen here is perhaps inverted: rather than a picture plane to service the multiple incarnations of the fragmented self, cult members shared a singular view of the self—one that was oddly unified by irrational, misguided, alien notions about life and death, television and spaceships. In their final days, their emotional connection to a comet outgrew their professional commitments in cyberspace. "They had escaped so much of America," Leon Wieseltier later commented in *The New Republic*, "but they had not escaped its thralldom of the screen."

Today, as design embraces methods and media beyond the purely two-dimensional, its phenomenological legacy—simply stated, its objective relationship to human experience—is informed not only by this broad panoply of social and aesthetic history, but also by certain formal conceits that derive as much from the parallel disciplines of film and painting as they do from design *per se*. Such an interdisciplinary reading—one that in spite of new media's largely "virtual" character considers its fundamental material contribution to the evolving theory and discipline of graphic design—has never been more critical.

: Minimalism/Maximalism:
The New Screen Aesthetic

When the history of new media is written a century from now, will critics describe these comparatively early, incunabula-esque days of the "modern" Internet like the French symbolist poet Arthur Rimbaud once did the modern city—as a perfect setting for a season in hell? Or are there likely to be advances in both theory and practice that suggest more promising aesthetic contributions to this emerging new discipline—contributions that will one day reflect the degree to which designers actually made a difference?

Increasingly, it seems, we may have good reason to be optimistic. Somewhere in the extensive experimental space of the digital hemisphere, designers are beginning to author, design, and engineer Websites that question the essential morphology of the screen in ways that skew our perceptual expectations. With advances in software plug-in integration now permitting more seamless cinematic representation online, they are dislocating the visual syntax of the screen and raising critical questions about the social and sensory dynamics of its multidimensional space. Today's most promising new media designers are probing that space intellectually, by reconsidering the presentation of content; they are testing it architecturally, by reassessing its compositional imperatives; and they are challenging it theatrically, by reorchestrating its multiple media components. Collectively, these experiments are pointing the way toward a new screen aesthetic that depends as much upon our understanding of design history as upon our willingness to forego previous conclusions about that history in order to welcome what might be, at long last, a new avant-garde. All of this is predicated on the basic notion that the screen succeeds best when understood as a balance of fundamentally opposing forces: it is all about the tension between structure and freedom.

There is, as it turns out, considerable historic precedent to substantiate this view. The emergence of twentieth-century modernism was essentially framed by similar tensions—from war to liberation, from economic depression to postwar optimism—and in the parallel

universe of aesthetic manufacture, from the restrained formal vocabularies of early modernist painting to the effusive reactionary backlash
of late abstract expressionism. For designers, these were fertile years in
what would come to be an emerging avant-garde, yet the trajectory of
modernism had an oddly bifurcated impact. On one hand were
staunch minimalists, disciples of the Bauhaus who advocated a kind of
pure, almost fetishistic formalism—a visual rhetoric borne of geometry, reduction, and reason. On the other were those whose love of
narrative and passion for varied, often lavish forms of visual expression would find equal representation in the emerging and increasingly
idiomatic imagery of the twentieth century. Each would participate in
and contribute to our critical understanding, today, of what graphic
design really is, deeply affecting its rich and often unruly definition.

Now, at the beginning of a new century, some of the most provocative visual explorations online are coming from sites that embrace a
fusion of both strains of modernism: these are sites that benefit at once
from the structured clarity of rational thinking and the capacity for
inventive, unorthodox (and often quite personal) expression. The first
is all about structure: indeed, the rigors of screen manufacture required
to bring a site to life—the meticulous coding, the complex engi-
neering—lend themselves quite naturally to certain practical design
choices, among them, pared-down type specifications; harmonious
grid systems; and balanced, if asymmetrical, compositional arrange-
ments. (Consider the streamlined formal codes of The New
Typography, Swiss Modernism and other enduring emblems of the
hygienic International Style. Think *minimalism*.) But the second, an
equally valid outgrowth of twentieth-century aesthetics, is all about
freedom: here, the designer is liberating a subjective point of view as an
enhanced expression of fact—not at the expense of it. Design in this
context is perhaps less pragmatic than pluralistic. (Consider the orna-
mental excesses of nineteenth-century chromolithography, the
exaggerated mannerisms of twentieth-century political caricature, or
the idiosyncratic composites of any of a number of postmodern
graphic assemblages. Think *maximalism*.)

Today, as design embraces methods and media beyond the purely
two-dimensional, its phenomenological legacy—quite simply, its
objective relationship to human experience—is informed not only by

this broad panoply of social and aesthetic history, but also by certain formal conceits that derive as much from the parallel disciplines of film and painting as they do from design *per se*. Such an interdisciplinary reading—one that in spite of new media's largely "virtual" character considers its fundamental material contribution to the evolving theory and discipline of graphic design—has never been more critical.

It is film, perhaps even more than painting, that deserves our attention now, given the increasingly dynamic opportunities for design on the computer screen. In the early days of pre-verbal cinema, the American poet Vachel Lindsay wrote extensively about the aesthetics of film language, comparing screen images to Egyptian hieroglyphs, action films to sculpture: he once defined crowd scenes as architecture in motion. (Lindsay's then-prescient observations offer a particularly apt analytical model to us today, as we consider these similarly "early" days of design on the "modern" Internet.) But what has been said of the actual screen space itself? Hugo Münsterberg, a noted Harvard psychologist before the First World War, was the first to attempt to define the architectonics of screen space, calling our attention to the meaning that certain camera movements can induce in our projection of depth onto the screened image. Such delicate psychological choreography is precisely what begins to happen on the Web: only here, instead of camera movements, it is mouse movements that induce meaning and trigger changes in visual dynamics which, in turn, affect our perception of screen depth. This assimilation of interactivity—quite literally, the idea that user input modifies screen display—fundamentally relocates the creative parameters within which design is both constructed and consumed. As paradigm shifts go, this one is seismic.

LOST IN SPACE

In the MonoCrafts "classic" site (www.yugop.com/ver2/) screen space is in continual flux: the user rolls over words to reveal pictures, pictures to reveal texts, navigational buttons to reveal kinetic constellations of dynamic matter, rather than static points of access. Screens perpetually redraw themselves to create animated interfaces that alternately conceal and reveal their content. A moving horizontal axis slices the main screen, giving birth to smaller, semi-translucent frames that resemble a floating filmstrip. Sub-navigation is presented as an annotation or an afterthought, a kind of expository text that fades in, on rollover, like a fleeting whisper. The pure formal language employed overall, however, is surprisingly restrained: It is orderly and monochromatic, geometric and spare. But present, too, is a strikingly lyrical component. In the main interface, a muted nature photograph appears in the background. In "Book of Typo-Beat" a disembodied keyboard is superimposed upon it—typing upon one's real keyboard displaces the screen keys, creating an abstracted typographic land-scape, a letterscape. Later, in "Nervous Matrix" the nature image subdivides into quadrants and refreshes as a series of aerial photo-graphs of urban grids. And throughout the site, an animation of blurred dot patterns—a cross between a German expressionist film and a study in molecular fission—swirls in a balletic haze while site components are loading. It is ethereal and boundless: screen space as graphic galaxy.

The newer version of the site (www.yugop.com/) adds subtle shifts in color gradation combined with floating typographic constel-lations to create even greater dimensionality, depth, and dreaminess. And it is dreamy—you meander laterally through these sites more than you browse them sequentially. The many lyrical "sitelets" ("Poetbot" for instance) accessible from MonoCrafts make streamlined navigation—the point A to point B kind—essentially impossible. Moreover, returning to the site in search of something you found a day before is often completely impossible. In addition, the use of a kind of elasticized rollover—in which dragging the mouse literally seems to stretch something on screen—produces a kind of disturbingly asynchronous vertigo. Like many sites that experiment with eye-hand-screen coordination, it is all about delayed reactions and suspended responsiveness, like your computer is experiencing the latent sensory lull of an antidepressant. It is digital Prozac.

The über-shockwaved Lessrain (www.lessrain.com) has a tighter response mechanism, yet rationalizes screen space in a similar way: Only here, instead of a black abyss, the arena of the screen is preternat-urally white. Perceptually, it is a wash: the absence of background color suggests an equally infinite territory. While there is less apparent kinetic activity (and sound) overall in this site, the main interface features a playful gavotte of cascading type that makes primary wayfinding a particular challenge. Navigation here is more straightforward: Tiny boxes that resemble a kind of futuristic morse code take you forward and backward across an essentially Cartesian axis. (The site is more a portfolio than the experimental MonoCrafts, and therefore benefits from a more linear underlying structure.) With such organizational parameters in place, the use and range of imagery here is delightfully eclectic, from a kind of Charles and Ray Eames-worthy photographic mise-en-scène to colorful video-game bots, animated oyster shells, and "Al in Wonderland," a modular photographic study that plays with the form of the fractal storyboard by juggling individual frames, modulating color values, and, ultimately, challenging the relationship between user input and narrative sequencing.

Like many experimental sites making use of plug-in capabilities, Lessrain.com suffers from a slow uptake: shockwave reloads interrupt cinematic flow and consequently inject an unpleasant note of technological mediation in an otherwise engaging series of visual explorations. It reminds us of the degree to which film—and increasingly, sound—provides the sensory glue enabling these design experiments to coalesce on our screens (and arguably, in our minds). But is that enough? The futurist painter Luigi Russolo once described film as needing to detach itself from reality in order to fulfill the evolution of painting. It may be that the opposite is true on the Web: Interactive media is social media. It needs to reaffirm its ties with reality and restore, perhaps, some of its more civilized conventions— the exchange of information, the reciprocity of language—in order to fully connect to the viewer. In the end, sites seem to fail when both information and imagery are awash in abstraction: conversely, they succeed when there is order to sustain the chaos. Avant-garde thinking aside, being lost in space is deliriously engaging as long as you know that at some point you can relocate yourself. Being lost indefinitely? That would be a hellish season, indeed.

The globally distributed media presence is the current multimedia publishing model of choice. It is easily reachable
and always accessible—on the street, on TV, online, on the brain.
It is largely founded on the supposition that ubiquity is the key
to achieving not only instant celebrity, but perhaps more
importantly, instant wealth. This essay looks at the ambitious
efforts of media hopefuls whose promises to embrace the
"multi" in multimedia demonstrates the rising value of
quantity over quality, as well as the uncertain role for design.

: Bigger, Better, Weirder: Age of the Behemoth

Forty days into a new century, American pharmaceutical giant Pfizer acquired American pharmaceutical giant Warner Lambert for a reported $90.2 billion. The British pharmaceutical giants Smith Kline Beecham and Glaxo Wellcome merged into a single $80.7 billion pharmaceutical giant. And America OnLine acquired Time Warner for the not-too-shabby sum of $165 billion. In a parallel gesture of entrepreneurial bravado, celebrity designer Ralph Lauren signed a thirty-year development deal with NBC Television to co-produce a series of media properties—including a Website and television show—in the familiar model of the aesthetically maniacal Martha Stewart, whose own aptly-titled "omnimedia" enterprise has redefined not only the economics of taste, but the notion, too, that one extremely driven person can become wildly successful across a veritable panoply of media. And then go public, and become even more successful.

Who wants to be a millionaire?

Never before in the popular press has the term "behemoth" been used with such alarming frequency. And one thing the behemoths do—and they do it quite well—is represent themselves as eminently capable of extending their reach, broadly speaking, everywhere you look. It is probably too early in the century to speculate about publishing trends, but it does seem that big is suddenly big, and that being big means being everywhere, and that being everywhere means having a "presence" that transcends independently defined media (such as print or TV) and blankets the world with—dare I say it?—a recognizeable *brand*.

This somewhat invasive notion of the globally distributed media presence is the current multimedia publishing model of choice. It is easily reachable and always accessible—on the street, on TV, online, on the brain. It is online/offline hybrids brimming with promotional gimmicks and backed by hefty stock inventory: search, surf, buy, and bask in the afterglow of this feel-good consumer experience so you can repeat the entire process fifteen minutes later without ever leaving the comfort of your chair.

The globally distributed media presence is largely founded on the supposition that ubiquity is the key to achieving not only instant celebrity, but perhaps more importantly, instant wealth. It is the newest abberation on the American Dream: fast and furious, Horatio Alger on steroids. How else to explain twenty-something CEOs and seven-figure corporate merger valuations? Or sudden IPOs emerging, and skyrocketing, from relative obscurity? Such epic turns of self-empowerment turn out to be almost spookily self-fulfilling. (Yale statistician and self-publishing magnate Edward Tufte is planning to host and produce his own television show. Need I say more?)

In the ongoing race to secure widespread "presence," perhaps the biggest gap lies between the computer screen and the TV screen. One is basically a repository of non-fiction, an environment framed by Boolean searches and deep-dish databases. The other is theatre in a box, a (typically) passive visual medium that is perhaps more concerned with ratings than with RAM. But as media converge and pipes get fatter, technology no longer makes such thematic distinctions necessary: a screen is just a screen. So media-presence seekers dream about developing "channels" which they cannot only use to distribute content, but with which they can reposition themselves as instant TV producers. Portal developer today, David E. Kelley tomorrow! To be fair, there are perhaps worse things to strive for: in 1999, *The Wall Street Journal* reported that the prolific Kelley signed a deal with Twentieth Century Fox TV that could make him the highest-paid producer in television history, earning more than $300 million over the course of the next six years.

Who wants to be a TV producer?

Ironically, such is the lure of overnight rags-to-riches success in the new economy that the once longed-for romantic status of the TV producer may itself be imperiled. With the rising popularity of game and "reality" shows, the episodic dramas and situation comedies that once lay claim to television's principal appeal find themselves on shaky ground. This in itself represents a significant paradigm shift not because it signals the death of scripted entertainment (though gainfully employed TV writers would tell you it does) but because it reveals the degree to which the empowerment of the individual has fundamentally galvanized our programming expectations, our viewing habits—and our basic level of taste.

Because this is an essay and not a philosophical treatise, I am forced by necessity to edit a more detailed trajectory of this illuminating revelation, but here is the abbreviated version. Let's assume that interactivity is a good thing, because it is fundamentally democratic. It empowers the individual to make choices, and allows those choices, in turn, to liberate desirable and relevant information. This is the hoped-for experience of a good search on a good search engine: the results at once reveal breadth (of options) and specificity (of choice). But now, if we divorce the results from the experience—and focus uniquely on the experience itself—we are left with an isolated and empowered searchaholic whose warped perception of the world lies in the exaggerated notion that he is one click away from anything he wants. Successful corporations and technology visionaries have parlayed this perception into kick-ass marketing opportunities: collaborative filtering, one-click shopping, and any number of logo-linked e-escutcheons amplify this illusion that life online is one big "world-is-my-oyster" opportunity. Ditto the well-executed "distributed presence" of a site with multiple merchandising options: amazon.com, at the top of its class with books, toys, auctions, and now even provenance-approved artifacts from Sothebys, has perfected the art of the screen-based, shop-till-you-drop media mall.

The psychological profile of The Empowered User is a personality type that has achieved unprecedented momentum in this new world. This explains the mystique of the game show, where average people have a chance to become contestants and contestants have a chance to become celebrities. The entire social order of digital life is, in a sense, reflected in this programming trend: hierarchy is diffused, the star system obliterated. In its place, The Empowered User becomes the center of the universe. It is me-generation vanity programming: like the passworded protocol of life on the Web, TV anonymity turns out to be an unusually powerful programming conceit.

Such is the conceptual premise behind MTV's "The Real World" and behind CBS-TV's "Big Brother," a series based on a successful Dutch program about a bunch of average people who share a house. (In a similar vein, McCann-Erickson's $150-million "mockumentary" ad campaign for The Microsoft Network illuminates the virtues of "the everyday Web" by featuring four strangers who share both a house and an MSN connection to the world.) In the non-stop spirit of 24x7 digital life, CBS ran "Big Brother" five nights a week, a scheduling move that, in a sense, distributes the show's presence throughout the week. Such blanket broadcasting represents the ever-growing ubiquity of the media presence model: it is a dramatically counterintuitive yet refreshingly daring move, and one that is virtually unprecedented in the programming of episodic television.

"Reality" programming has its roots in the fibers of the online vernacular: the chatrooms, the bulletin boards, the community inter-action that can (and should) be traced back as far as The WeLL. This sort of empowerment—the ability to globally connect likeminded individuals through simple, accessible means—remains one of the Internet's most laudable assets. It is the magnification of that oppor-tunity and the unfortunate self-aggrandizement that comes with it that mistakenly promotes the notion of screen presence as an infi-nitely scaleable commodity. And in the endless real estate of the Web, there appear to be no concerns about supply and demand: you do not have to be Martha Stewart or Ralph Lauren or Glaxo Wellcome or Time Warner to have an online presence. But it probably doesn't hurt.

Increasingly, "presence" is being defined as broadly as possible, distributed across media platforms from television to magazines to PDAS to IMAX Films. Publishing models—which were once defined by circulation numbers and paperback rights—have now become equally, well, behemoth-like. America Online buying Time Warner? Enough said. But it is also the era of digital shrinkage: the popularity of handheld devices alone has raised the ante for the miniaturization of published content. From email to e-books, designers are being asked to consider how the integrity of what they do might extend to the microscopic screen: WAP (or Wireless Application Protocol) technology is the *lingua franca* of this new orbit. And conceptually, it is about as far from the spirit of the behemoth enterprise as it is possible to go.

Who wants to be a designer?

There is something deeply troubling in the discrepancy between the accelerated growth of the economy in general and the fundamental myopia required to perform this laborious task—evidence of an emerging cultural divide between The Big Real World and the tiny design world. If a broadly defined distributed presence across multiple media is the publishing model of the new century, then what can be said of editing a book, or a Website, or the main titles for a feature film onto a Palmtop, or a mobile phone, or a wristwatch? Is design only concerned with what happens between Ralph Lauren on a sweater . . . and Ralph Lauren on a screen?

Admittedly, publishing models are made, not born: and so, it must be remembered, are the current crop of media millionaires. I am not advocating the importance of accruing wealth or achieving stardom so much as the danger of being shoved half a dozen notches down the evolutionary food chain, because instead of contributing the breadth of our experience to integrated forms of content management, we are busy rendering teeny, tiny, bitmapped screens of WAP data. Instead of questioning the political value or editorial meaning or basic validity of a distributed media presence, we are struggling to iron out the wrinkles between technologies that threaten the integrity of the way things look. At the dawn of the age of the behemoth, this strikes me as an extremely small view of the world.

An audience, by its very nature, is a dynamic entity, not a static body. Its permutations—across time, space, and media platforms—make it fundamentally impossible to quantify. Because they presuppose a static viewership, audience measurement tactics are, therefore, inevitably doomed to failure: audiences (read people) are remarkably difficult to meter. This essay looks at existing models for media measurement and examines the unresolved relationships between spectatorship and sponsorship, between author and audience, between what we watch and, more importantly perhaps, how we watch it.

Some years ago, a professor of mine went to his dentist to have his teeth drilled.

"So!" inquired the dentist. "How's commercial art?"

Insulted at the insinuation that he, a serious, trained graphic designer, would be considered in the same category as, say, a sign painter, the professor looked the dentist squarely in the eye. "So!" sneered the professor. "How's dental hygiene?"

I offer this anecdote for two reasons: first, I have never met a graphic designer who did not bristle at the assumption that graphic design and commercial art are one and the same (they are not), and second, because somewhere out there, there is a media research firm eager to categorize us as one and the same (we are not).

This proves, quite simply I think, why demographics are misleading. However, such statistics routinely provide cues for selling time and space to advertisers who want to reach particular types of people: these are what is known as target audiences. It is widely believed that target audiences can be determined and subsequently reached through such research, which suggests that they—which is to say we—can be measured.

A chilling thought, indeed.

Much has been written about methods of measuring audience response, and this is perhaps nowhere more compelling a notion than in the minds (and pocketbooks) of prospective advertisers, though it might arguably be said that designers are just as preoccupied with this particularly over-fetishized aspect of contemporary culture: addressing the interests of one's audience is, after all, central to the designer's process. But advertising complicates this—perhaps even corrupts it. Advertisers in particular have long invested considerable amounts of effort into hiring media research groups to determine the most accurate ways of measuring and selling to their public. Over time, data collection methods have grown to include everything from diaries to interviews to telephone recall to personal metering, all ways of taking a kind of collective pulse of the public's viewing habits, one individual (or household) at a time. Such extensive—and invasive—research efforts typically target particular demographic groups in the interest of gaining a more accurate understanding of that audience's viewing habits and, by conjecture, its assumed patterns of consumption. "Sell good things, things that people should have, and sell them with dignity—and taste," Deborah Kerr purrs to Clark Gable in the film *The Hucksters*. "That's a career for any man, a career to be proud of."

Today, the very notion of a targeted demographic is as outmoded as this film. The sheer abundance of programming options on television—or site offerings on the Web—have led to a fragmentation not only among audiences themselves but also of the viewing habits that characterize them. Moreover, the notion of "demographic tonnage"—lumping viewers together by age, race, and gender—denies the subtle, idiosyncratic details that often make for the most engaging ideas and, not surprisingly, some of the most successful ad campaigns.

Demographics are dangerous. To define an audience in such terms is to constrain its proportions: an audience, by its very nature, is a dynamic entity, not a static body. Its permutations—across time, space, and media platforms—make it fundamentally impossible to quantify. Because they presuppose a static viewership, audience measurement tactics are, therefore, inevitably doomed to failure. The simple truth is this: audiences do not sit still.

And therein lies the problem.

Of course, audiences used to sit still. Long before the days of the Walkman, media were no more portable than a refrigerator. Radios and TVs were domestically bound, stationary objects that transmitted from a fixed spot in the home. Programs were live, not prerecorded, and often relied on the support of a single advertiser—a sponsor, whose name appeared with some frequency during the broadcast, often in the form of evangelical endorsements delivered by wooden spokespersons whose task it was to proselytize on the virtues of a vacuum cleaner or the delights of a new car. Often, the line between the program and the ad was blurred. Viewers did not seem to care: they sat, and they watched. *Passively.*

Then they went out and spent money. *Actively.*

The cause-and-effect dynamic of spectatorship and spending found its ideal incarnation in televised media. On screen, unlike radio, products could be shown in use, which proved to be an enormously persuasive sales tool. Then, in the early 1950s, Procter and Gamble—the American manufacturer of such well-known household products as Tide laundry soap and Top Job linoleum cleaner—introduced a series of half-hour television dramas that were punctuated exclusively with ads for their products, thus selling to the very segment of the audience that would presumably purchase them. In other words, they created programming for their ads, rather than running ads during other peoples' programs.

Looking back, this was a comparatively radical advertising idea: to create an entire new genre of programming geared to a particular demographic, in this case, women between the ages of eighteen and forty-nine. If one considers the invention of "banners"—those dull, unimaginative rectangles that sit at the periphery of most Web-pages—these early soap operas (as they have come to be known) were, at least in a conceptual sense, utterly revolutionary for their day. And within this type of controlled viewership, an increase in product sales could be directly tied to the size (and loyalty) of this particular target audience.

Despite the fragmentation that characterizes contemporary viewership, the economics of broadcast advertising continue to rely heavily on such evidence. This is the focus of statistical ratings which, in the u.s. for example, break the nation into 211 separate markets and track television use by time and by network. Like ABG in Britain, the u.s. based Nielsen Company is the king of evaluating programs and commercials via precisely such ratings. Simply put, Nielsen ratings provide an estimate of audience size and composition for television programmers and commercial advertisers and are, it is widely believed, a barometer of the public's viewing habits. Nielsen collects data from local and national pools through something they call the "People Meter" (another chilling thought). People Meters are placed in roughly 5,000 homes and are used to record two things: what is being watched and who is watching. Whenever the television set is turned on a red light flashes from time to time on the meter, reminding viewers to press their assigned button to indicate if they are watching television. (Additional buttons are available for guest use.) Nielsen Media Research also provides information about competitive advertising expenditures and audience reach for print, radio, and television as well as information about computer usage and traffic on the Internet. Theirs is a virtual monopoly in media surveillance: Nielsen is to media measurement what Kleenex is to tissue paper.

The good news is, Nielsen's reach is comprehensive: while television itself boasts about a ninety-nine percent national penetration rate (cable TV is in about sixty-two percent of all U.S. homes while home computers—only a fraction of which are wired to the Internet—are in just about a third) Nielsen knows who is out there, what they are watching, and when they are watching it. The bad news is, audience measurement continues to be a remarkably inexact science. And despite half a century of technological advances since its inception, measurement protocols and data collection methods remain surprisingly primitive and are, consequently, eminently prone to failure.

For example, four times a year, (during what are known as the "sweeps" months) additional demographic viewing data is collected, in which members within a Nielsen household are asked to keep a diary for one week, recording their viewing habits in quarter-hour increments. It is estimated that Nielsen hand-processes over one million of these diaries each year: not surprisingly, perhaps, mistakes happen somewhere in the handoff. Recently, an error in data entry for WXXA (the Fox Network affiliate in Albany, New York) boasted fictitious ratings that resulted in $400,000 to $500,000 of unearned advertising revenue. (One household of nine adults had submitted a viewing report stating each watched an average of 13.5 hours of television per day, most of it on WXXA.) Such concentrated viewing throws the projections, skews the demographics, and compromises the very believability of the system itself.

Of course, not all audience research is flawed: what fails are broad-based studies that make collective assumptions about viewership as though it is a singular, static activity. Conversely, more focused research, within more controlled conditions, can occcasionally reveal significant findings about the way we look at things. Consider, for example, the Eye-Trac studies, introduced in the mid-1980s by Mario Garcia and Pegie Stark at the Poynter Institute for Media Studies, an editorial think-tank in St. Petersburg, Florida. Looking at prototypical newspapers from three different cities, Garcia and Stark attached video cameras to headbands of a select group of readers and examined where the readers' eyes moved to when they read. When the videos were later analyzed, it became immediately evident that, contrary to public opinion, people did not automatically look at the "lead story" in the top right corner of a page. Instead, they found readers' eyes gravitated first to the strongest visual: a photograph, an illustration, even a headline. This type of research illuminated the value of design in determining editorial hierarchies and, consequently, in directing an audience's attention. And because it was tested within a print environment, the controlled circumstances of such a study were more easily measured.

Reading is, at least in a physical sense, a more stationary activity. But watching TV evokes entirely different behaviors. Even though the screen itself is static, our interaction with it is not: we flip the channels, mute the sound, record when we are not home. Audiences (read people) are remarkably difficult to meter. And what relationship—if any— does what they watch have to what they buy? And who are "they," anyway? In a campaign that brilliantly ridiculed the false statistical readings claimed by broadcasters, advertisers, and media research mavens, the British advertising agency Howell, Henry, Chaldecott, and Lury ran a controversial advertisement some years ago in the *Financial Times* that showed a man and a woman making love in front of a television set. "Current advertising says these people are watching your ad," read the headline. "Who's really getting screwed?"

Though much has been said of the discrepancy between information and knowledge, what has not been examined is the degree to which visual cues—what we might have once characterized as design decisions—contribute to the perceptual contrivances that frame our daily media experiences. This new reality is, in fact, more surreal than real. Using Daniel Boorstin's notion of "pseudo-events" as an analytical model, this essay looks at the degree to which the pseudo has overtaken the real, blurring the line between taped and live, physical and phony.

When President Clinton's four-hours-and-three-minutes of video-taped Grand Jury testimony were broadcast on television in the autumn of 1998, nearly twenty-three million of us watched. The media attention generated by this lamentable situation was dramatically disproportionate to its political significance: in other words, the suspense overwhelmed the specifics, consequently blurring the line between fact, fallacy, and pure fiction. Debate over questions of presidential misconduct (abuse of power, perjury, and lies) and prosecutorial misconduct (abuse of power, perjury, and lies) fueled countless additional hours of talk show TV, feeding our insatiable hunger for a kind of self-perpetuating, tautological media engine: just the same-old, same-old packaged—indeed, branded—in new and different ways. Throughout the saga and its wildly protracted denouement, we were bombarded by evocative descriptions, repetitive images, claims both accusatory and exculpatory, threats of impeachment and rumors of resignation. The public consensus was that this intrusive media inquisition would reveal the truth. Or at least that it would reveal, well, *something*.

And yet, despite the stir caused by the White House scandal, more than three times as many people—seventy-nine million viewers worldwide—tuned into the final episode of "Seinfeld" the previous spring. The degree to which this show, a situation comedy, was publically mourned and indeed, eulogized represents an even more disheartening truth: it was a show that prided itself on the fact that it was about *nothing*.

In both cases, we were mesmerized not only by the events, but by the orbit of media miscellany—the talk shows, the magazines, the gossip—that surrounded them. We remain slaves to round-the-clock media, addicted to the images they project, the idealized, romanticized, dramatized renditions of ourselves, our heroes and our enemies, crystallizations of our seemingly endless stream of material fetishes. Through technology we are at once empowered and imprisoned by these images, needing and believing in them more than we may care to admit. The media excels in its celebration of such hype, in all its virtual, sensational, inescapable glory.

Hype, of course, is no stranger to the media. In a recent Gallup poll in which audiences were asked to name the media outlets they trusted the most, television newsmagazines (a TV sub-genre spawned by the birth of "Nightline" during the 1981 Iran hostage crisis) topped the list at a whopping fifty-one percent. Print newspapers (at thirty-seven percent) and print newsmagazines (twenty-seven percent) were believed to be the least reliable sources of information.

Here in the era of televised media, verisimilitude reigns supreme, hype is hip, and pictures speak much, *much* louder than words. "We'd rather watch you on television than talk to you," observed playwright Sam Shepard in an recent interview. "Just get rid of you altogether and make you an image."

SIMULATING REALITY: SPIN AND THE PSEUDO EVENT

Nearly forty years ago, the noted historian (and former Librarian of Congress) Daniel Boorstin wrote critically of something he termed "pseudo-events": namely, the counterfeit simulations in everyday life that were replacing the authentic with the contrived. Boorstin warned against what he called "the menace of unreality," arguing his essential point with penetrating insight: that we seek simulations because we are not satisfied with reality, and that ideals were being replaced by superficial images. Boorstin was not alone in his thinking (Baudrillard, among others, warned against "substituting signs of the real for the real itself") though his were comparatively early and indeed, prescient observations that feed directly into what we have come to think of, in today's world, as "spin": the buzz or frenzy surrounding a person or event that swirls into a haze of media hype, submerging the original event or person in a fog of overwhelming— and overabundant—detail. From threats of disclosure (the future of the Presidency) to gobs of over-exposure (the end of "Seinfeld"), we thirst for truth (did Clinton lie under oath?) and lust for closure (how will the last episode of "Seinfeld" conclude?). The line between fiction and non-fiction gets murkier, making it fundamentally impossible to distinguish reality from illusion. Technology compounds these hazards, adding a plethora of choices, though not necessarily contributing to any clearer understanding of what it is we are choosing, or more importantly, why.

Reality itself is on shaky ground, a chaotic sampling of splintered messages and fleeting images, juxtaposed by their multiple appearances in various types of media, blurring the distinction between taped and live, physical and phony. Time is cyclical, space is virtual: it is the age of the continuous replay. Whether we are watching footage of O. J. Simpson's white runaway van careening along the highway, or of Mark McGwire's record-breaking seventy home runs, events happen and are instantly eclipsed by their reportage.

Today, it seems, we do not merely seek simulations, we create them. Certainly as designers, it might even be argued that we willingly participate in their manufacture. Notes Boorstin: "By a diabolical irony, the very facsimiles of the world which we make on purpose to bring it within our grasp, to make it less elusive, have transported us into a new world of blurs. By sharpening our images we have blurred all our experience." And more and more, despite the fact that opportunities for information access grow more plentiful by the second, the opportunities for fact-finding, or truth-seeking, or knowledge-building grow dimmer. Whether we are augmenting reality through electronic means (consider the wonders of High Definition TV, where you can peruse headlines, download stock quotes and watch "Bewitched" reruns all at once) or manipulating reality through scientific means (consider the promises of biotechnology, where you might choose the sex of your next child—or simply clone the last one) we are stretching, scripting, morphing, manipulating, and, true to Boorstin's prophecy, simulating reality by willingly choosing the synthetic over the authentic. "The danger," observes cultural critic James Glassman, a fellow at the American Enterprise Institute, "is that the pseudo drives out the real."

In our effort to embrace virtuality as an acceptable social condition, the futuristically inclined among us have gone one step further. In today's world of media sensurround, the pseudo is the real.

PLAYING WITH REALITY: THE WORLD ACCORDING TO ME
The typical screen interface is game-like to the extreme. The Web, our

window to the Internet, is filled with buttons and arrows and blinking lights and flashing icons: like a flattened video arcade (and despite the effort taken to bevel the edges of the buttons, it is indeed a flatland), the "experience" is essentially a playful one. It is your turn: what will you do? Where will you go? Customized interfaces further flatten the screen by packing in vast (and frequently unnecessary) quantities of information—scrolling lists, drop-down menus—suggesting a graphic complexity which is sometimes puzzling and frequently para-lyzing. Such customization is a particular conceit of the Internet, where service providers struggle to increase traffic (and boost commerce) by playing to the narcissism of a decentralized public, offering endless variations on what technology soothsayer Nicholas Negroponte calls the "Daily Me": thus *MyYahoo, MyNetscape* and even, God help us, *MyAOL.*

And now—coming soon—what might as well be called My TV: a New and Improved *übermedium* that promises to revolutionize the way we watch television—and use the computer—by streamlining their convergent introduction into our homes. High Definition Television (or HDTV) is a new broadcast technology predicated on a system that replaces analog data with digital data, thus enabling broadcasters to transmit more stuff alongside its classic programming options: an entire edition of a newspaper, sports scores, or stock market quotes, for instance. It is a new way of transmitting program-ming material, with better picture and sound quality, more detail, and more implied interaction with the public. By combining enhanced image quality with customized information options, HDTV touts itself as the ultimate in high-tech one-stop shopping. Certainly the hyper-clarity of the digital signal itself suggests an even greater potential for screen addiction. "HDTV colors … make the eye dance and sing," reports *Village Voice* art critic Peter Schjeldahl. "It throws the optic nerve into overdrive and keeps it there."

But wait! As if this visual lure were not enough, there is the added empowerment of augmenting a televised experience by controlling its visual direction. "In some cases," boasts a recent report issued by the Mass Media Bureau of the Federal Communications Commission, "viewers will be able to select camera angles."

Hello?

What happens when point-of-view becomes a transferable commodity? Why can't news just be news, or entertainment just entertainment? Must it be commandeered, appropriated and made into a participatory act in order to be appreciated, understood, remembered? Here, it is not only the line between fact and fiction which blurs, but the line between fact and interpretation, and, moralistic as it might seem, between right and wrong.

Though much has been said of the discrepancy between information and knowledge, what has not been examined is the degree to which visual cues—what we might have once characterized as design decisions (only they are everyone's decisions now)—contribute to such contrivances. When designed and edited and composed with dramatic intent—teasers and bumpers on TV, *schlockwaved* animations on the Web and now, customized camera angling—there is an implicit corruption taking place. This new reality is, in fact, more surreal than real. "It's going to be both scary and great," notes Schjeldahl, "especially when artistic people have had time to fool around with the possibilities." Scary to think that creative direction can have such critical and, indeed, ethical consequences.

As the pseudo overtakes the real, it is precisely such "possibilities" which cloud the content. Consider a typical evening news broadcast in New York, in which an in-depth feature on welfare mothers (or global warming, or presidential impeachment) follows a made-for-TV movie on the same subject. Up go the ratings—but is it ethical? Now imagine you are controlling the camera angle: what now? Such sensationalism may be fueled by the technological capacities of HDTV, but the ethics, and the editorial judgments that frame them, remain seriously in question. Falsely dramatic signals send erroneous messages to an unsuspecting, if attentive, audience. Implicit in the creation of those signals are the millions of visual details—suggestive, speculative and most of all, seductive—that keep us coming back for more.

If the current trend in media consumption is to praise user-driven interaction above all else, then what value can we place on pre-selected systems, delivered to the public in pre-conceived formats? It is not enough to say that print media is an antiquated medium: what of the editorial process that supports it, and of the judgments that typically define its tone, its value and—from a design perspective—its material presence in our culture? This essay suggests that while prescribed hierarchy may be the enemy of the electronic age, it remains a fundamentally critical editorial tool in the design of both printed and electronic matter.

: The Dynamics of Choice and the Death of Hierarchy

In November of 1997, as the American press alerted its citizens to the possibility of incipient attack by the Iraqis, reports rolled in with accounts of the healthy birth of septuplets in Iowa. These news stories—one terrifying and political, one miraculous and biological—alternately gripped the nation in the days that followed, as the media volleyed back and forth with warnings of impending annihilation one moment and the wonders of fertility treatments the next. Was this merely a twisted reflection on the uneventful progress between the Clinton administration and the United Nations—and the Iraqi delegates with whom they wrestled? A way to diffuse the tension, to animate the proceedings—quite frankly, to change the subject? Or a way to hint at the dueling progress between stories (Were the babies off the ventilators yet? Had the President secured a peace agreement yet?) by intercutting between two such disparate chronicles of emerging life on the one hand, and imminent destruction on the other? Or was it merely a wanton display of the media's apparent glee in getting a jump start on the Christmas season by reporting an edge-of-your-seat human interest story, even as hard news sometimes took a back seat?

The answer is: none of the above, but why? Because the egalitarian nature of this *pas-de-deux* reportage enabled these stories to reveal themselves almost exclusively in parallel, to the point where the front page of *The New York Times* ran photographs of President Clinton, Sadaam Hussein, and the septuplets' father side-by-side—and exactly the same size. (Actually, it was merely the headshots that were the same size: the actual photograph of the babies' father ran considerably larger.) Such compositional decisions would lead the average reader to quickly conclude that neither story took precedence over the other—and despite the lesser-known fact that the *Times* typically runs its lead story in the narrow right-hand column on the front page, this clearly appeared to be the case. In this particular instance, the very decision to abandon size and placement conventions in favor of the equality with which these two diametrically-opposed stories were presented raises important questions about the role of design, the function of hierarchy, and the future of information access in an electronic democracy.

In most major newspapers, so-called "hierarchy" itself is fundamentally driven by the newsworthiness of key stories, and the decisions regarding their choice and presentation are typically made by news editors—not, it should be noted, by designers. It used to be that such formatting—which typically involved a prioritization of content and an explicit articulation of the kinds of visual hierarchies that would make complex information clear—was, in fact, the great contribution of the designer. But today, in an age in which the average plugged-in individual can seek and retrieve highly specialized (even customized) information, such prioritized news judgments no longer seem quite so relevant. What is striking is the degree to which such advances—and indeed, disturbances—in information delivery have themselves led to new perceptual expectations in the print realm. Could the loss of hierarchy on the front page of *The New York Times* be a direct consequence of this, the rise of the personal, electronic, and hierarchy-free news transmittal?

In a culture that values the individual, prizes independence, and celebrates the dynamics of free choice, it might be easy to conclude that such classic definitions of hierarchy are tantamount to fascism. But if the current trend in media consumption is to praise user-driven interaction above all else, then what value can we place on pre-selected, pre-ordained systems, delivered to the public in pre-conceived formats? It is not enough to say that the newspaper (or for that matter, the magazine) is an antiquated medium: what of the editorial process that supports it, and of the judgments that typically define its tone, its value and—from a design perspective—its material presence in our culture?

In recent years, the trend in newspaper design has been to create multiple points of entry (think datelines and pull-quotes) to facilitate the quick scan and thereby service the time-pressed reader. Such design decisions clearly presuppose the option of entering at any point, itself an "interactive"—and anti-hierarchical—gesture. This is an issue of particular significance on Websites, where readers have the option of clicking where (and when) they like. What is striking is that as we grow more accustomed to dwelling in such hyperkinetic digital worlds, our expectations—and indeed, our demands—for information access in print appear to be undergoing a radical shift. And while a good deal has been written about speed and fragmentation and their consequent impact on communication design, the flip side of this shift is equally if not more significant: without hierarchy to designate the visual drama of information on a single (and static) surface, the result is often a flat wasteland of ill-defined content. And while prescribed hierarchy may be the enemy of the electronic age, it remains a fundamentally critical editorial tool in the design of both printed and electronic matter. Moreover, its value as an instrument of journalistic integrity cannot be undersold, let alone eliminated.

Taken to an extreme, of course, hierarchy is a rather tacit form of fascism. As an organizational principle, it suggests a kind of dictatorial, impregnable, and unilateral set of parameters. It designates boundaries and rules. It drives the reader—the reader does not drive it. It is the complete antithesis of free choice, and thus flies in the face of what might broadly be characterized as democratic principle. Yet on some very fundamental level, hierarchy is a function of irrefutable logic. It illuminates meaning and establishes relative importance. It rallies against stasis, against monotony, and visual boredom. It rationalizes vast amounts of seemingly unrelated data, providing order and structure, giving a tangible shape to the otherwise chaotic, disenfranchised nature of things. The establishment of hierarchy, in the hands of a good designer, is proof of the validity of good design: it is a kind of visual choreography, but proportioned to the page—not the stage—and poised to maintain a balance between readability (structure) and delight (freedom).

Conversely, the loss of hierarchy results in a kind of cultural monotony that is itself antithetical to the kind of variety we crave from life—and arguably, from design as well. Such monotony is often perceived as its own editorial straitjacket: deep . . . or dull? A good example might be the recent proliferation of "themed" issues published in the u.s. by such variety-based publications as *The New Yorker* (which released special issues over the past year covering topics including fashion, fiction, and most recently, cartoons) and *The New York Times Magazine* (ditto, on such über-themes as technology and religion). In these publications, sameness overrides structure, the classic front-of-the-book versus back-of-the-book orientation virtually disappearing beneath a fog of stories positioning multiple viewpoints against an allegedly shared editorial gestalt.

Here, the notion of hierarchy, which once aimed to establish a kind of lateral balance on a single surface, seems to be edging toward a deeper (if not more myopic) editorial substrate—and again, is perhaps excessively influenced by its great and obstreperous competitor, the screen. In the screen-based environment, sustained readership is measured in "click-throughs"—though in truth, a more accurate term might be "clock-throughs" since many Web publishers seem more concerned with duration (of visits) than with depth (of penetration). What remains significant is the degree to which hierarchy in nested spaces (like the Web) is achieved through layered—not lateral—presentation, and how such revised hierarchical practice is affecting, for better or worse, the ways we consider the printed page.

Unlike the finite spatial parameters of the page, the Web offers unlimited real estate. Here there is no need to edit and shape material the way we must in print. Once, such editing was considered a challenge: we used less (fewer words, less stuff) to say more. If this trend is reversing, it is especially apparent in many magazines: this is one environment in which we do judge a book by its cover. And yet many consumer magazines—which typically rely on cover lines to sell copies at the newsstand—seem to be abandoning editorial decision-making by running a plethora of cover copy that often appears to say (and sell) everything at the expense of saying (and selling) something. Are publishers likely to reach more readers by offering something for everyone? Or does this unstructured cacophony of type diminish the value of, say, teasing a lead story and promoting a committed editorial point-of-view?

Point-of-view used to be precisely what sold newspapers and magazines: you subscribed to a particular publication because you valued the opinions of its editors and contributors. Yet today, the premium is on the everyman rather than the expert, a notion that virtually nullifies the space between author and audience, between publisher and public. Increasingly, it seems, in an environment of unlimited options, the voice of experience is consensus-based—not specialist-based.

Consider this example: on the Internet, collaborative filtering is a new and increasingly popular technology in which users answer detailed questionnaires reflecting their opinions and tastes on a particular topic. The system then reciprocates by offering advice gleaned from the pooled replies of other users. Thus, a food site that asks users to rate culinary delights will likely compile its collective data, and return suggestions—if you like crème brulée, you'll love charlotte russe. Such statements are based on the purely anecdotal opinions retrieved from an unlimited number of anonymous, faceless, amateur food critics. Where is the editorial judgment? Why would you listen to these people? How can this possibly be a richer or more rewarding experience than reading M. F. K. Fisher or Patricia Wells or Jonathan Meades?

Collaborative filtering illuminates the current misguided notion that values quantity over quality. This—perhaps quite literally—is the ultimate casualty of the digital age and arguably, of our hierarchy-free society. With technology comes decentralized power and with it, greater personal freedom and enhanced choice. That such decentralization also subverts the sorts of hierarchies that previously led to deeper and more enlightened understanding is perhaps a greater loss to modern civilization than any of us care to acknowledge.

This essay looks at a new kind of illiteracy: encouraged by the widespread pluralism that so indelibly colors contemporary culture on the one hand, and forgiven by the extraordinary impulse to self-publish that dominates it on the other. It skewers the loose, anything-goes expressionism that has emerged as the prevailing style of so much networked media: messy and myopic, part stand-up comedy and part soapbox-proselytizing, a "medium" that is more likely to ricochet from personal issues than respond to public ones, raising critical questions about authorship, editing, and the consequent tensions presented by and for the design professions.

Over the past decade or so, there have been occasional rumblings within the design profession suggesting that certification—quite literally, the requirement that designers be licensed to practice—would be a good thing. From the beginning, its detractors protested vociferously: how could professional design qualifications actually be assessed? Would we be expected to dutifully memorize 150,000 Pantone colors, for instance, or to correctly pronounce *The Hypnerotomachia Poliphili?* It soon became clear that while the mechanics of design were measurable, many of its more elusive aspects—like, say, talent—were, in fact, much more difficult to quantify. And since bad design rarely qualifies as malpractice (there are of course exceptions, and you know who you are), the implementation of actual regulations soon proved a futile pursuit.

In the absence of such tangible criteria for excellence, and with the rise of new technologies permitting more, shall we say, democratic access to the tools of our trade, the standards for what even constitutes design have become exceedingly relaxed. Politically, this kind of freedom of expression is generally understood to be quite promising: it presupposes a progressively libertarian view of the world, freed from the shackles of rulemaking and restrictiveness (not to mention a welcome release from paste-up, production details, and the exigencies of good penmanship). But in practicality, this new, broadly-defined world is not so much libertarian as libertine. One need only look at the indulgent, shameless, even profligate materials being posted on Websites around the world—punctuation-free, design-challenged, and awash in typos—to understand that while certification may not necessarily be the answer, a return to a few basic design principles might be a very good thing, indeed.

But design principles are not the real problem here. The deeper, more resonant issue is the degree to which we have come to accept this sort of ill-defined, anything-goes expressionism: messy and myopic, part stand-up comedy and part soapbox-proselytizing, a "medium" (if it can even be called that) that is more likely to ricochet from personal issues than respond to public ones, and one that, in the end, verges on illiteracy. This is a new kind of illiteracy, encouraged by the widespread pluralism that colors contemporary culture on the one hand, and forgiven by the extraordinary impulse to self-publish that dominates it on the other. More often than not, the new illiteracy is an incubator for anger, a breeding ground for self-importance—the world according to me, me, me. Undisciplined in form and irreverent in tone, its denizens play by their own rules, invent their own taxonomies, and espouse their own highly individualized view of the universe. "i know i'm starting to get really sloppy in my sentences," opines a young designer in an online discussion group, "but i'm kinda rushing while i write this cuz i gotta get to school." The intentional use of childlike grammar here— the "kinda" and "gotta" and horrifyingly precious misspelling of the word "cuz"—is nothing compared to the warped perception of inflated self-worth evidenced in this writer's final posting: "i'm gonna write a book."

On the Web, the opportunity to say anything is both seductive and eminently achievable. Consequently, the obligation to edit oneself is apparently nonexistent. Taste aside (and principles of good design would qualify, I think, as taste in this context) the sorts of things being said and done on Websites around the world suggest, as media critic Jon Katz once observed, "more freedom of the press than anyone ever dared imagine." These range from a designer I know who has chosen to publicly voice his unmitigated anger toward his former employers (his ludicrous homepage shows a pathetically lame stab at grunge-lyricism that has taken the form of a more general swipe at the entire design profession), to a stay-at-home mom who has created a Website for stay-at-home moms that is all about fury and indignation about being a stay-at-home mom. Both seem intentionally *badly* designed, complete with interminable downloads, undecipherable type and vibrating colors as if to say: I'm angry, and my site says I'm angry too, so don't mess with me.

This use of site-as-therapy-tool is not uncommon: what is interesting is the way design is used to advance its position. Whether prompted by anger, evangelism, or, as Michael Rock so eloquently wrote in a recent issue of *Emigre*, "piety peddling," the idea that the democracy of the Web enables such constitutional rights to find visual form is neither surprising nor inappropriate. Yet while this kind of open-minded diversity may seem encouraging in a sociological sense, it is also fundamentally dystopian in both its exalted claims of superiority and its tacit contributions to what becomes, at least aesthetically, a rather diminished quality of life. (Angry Websites make people feel good: but are they good for people?) Pluralism, in the context of Web publishing (and given the enormity of its infinitely scalable genre) may be chic, but it is really the ultimate cop-out. At its best, it is multicultural, geographically diverse, and philosophically eclectic. At its worst, it is garbage that becomes garbage because there are simply no barriers to entry. It is pluralism run amok. And this, I would posit, is *not* a good thing.

In his epic book, *The Civilization of Illiteracy,* author Mihai Nadin argues that it is precisely this pluralism that allows for multiple literacies, no longer tied to our classic definitions of text-based, unidirectional learning. "In this world," Nadin writes, "many new literacies, of shorter duration, override the need and possibility of one encompassing literacy…the new literacies provide means for human interaction appropriate to achieving probably the most radical forms of individualism and the most intriguing means of social interaction." Nadin's optimism echoes the findings of Harvard education guru Howard Gardner, whose theory of "multiple intelligences" has revolutionized learning practices throughout the world (Gardner's books have been translated into twenty languages). His theory is predicated on the notion that our culture—and schools—teach, test, reinforce, and primarily reward two kinds of intelligence: intelligence that is verbal (linguistic) and intelligence that is logical (or mathematical). Gardner has added other kinds of intelligence—he calls them "languages"—that cut through cultural, educational, and ability differences, among them visual (spatial) intelligence; physical (kinesthetic, or athletic) intelligence: musical, interpersonal, intrapersonal intelligence; and, most recently, naturalist intelligence. Advocates of education reform see Gardner's theories as transformative and indeed, liberating. Of course they are. They are also safe, non-confrontational, and deliriously diplomatic.

So basically, the message is this: there are no rules. Anybody can do, say, be anything. Design principles—like good sentence structure, editing techniques, or the ability to articulate an original idea—seem to have little if any tangible value here. Recently, I came upon a syllabus for a course in advanced interaction design, being taught at a distinguished American university (hint: it is in Silicon Valley) and focusing on "experience design." "Since everyone has experience with experiences," explains the pious instructor, "every student should already be qualified to learn more about applying what they implicitly understand to the problems of creating, 'interactive media.'" It is not clear to me exactly which, if any, of Gardner's "intelligences" are at play here, but the idea that "experience" qualifies as a sufficient prerequisite for an advanced university-level design course leads me to believe that those advocates of education reform might just be barking up the wrong tree.

What is disconcerting about this wave of unbridled permissiveness is a fundamental inability to distinguish between self-experience and broader, more culturally polymorphous experience. (Something, arguably, designers used to do pretty well.) The Web, as a publishing platform, makes such distinctions seem arcane and unnecessary. But if we assume, for a moment, that design is perhaps obliged to identify broader communication needs to a wider audience, such qualifications may, in fact, be more critical than ever.

Instead, what is happening is that along with the relaxed standards and forgiving criteria that circumscribe our daily media-making (and taking) habits, we have gradually lowered the standards for our general viewing expectations. And this dumbing-down is not only happening on the Web: today's television viewers, by all indications, seem to prefer the new man-on-the-street reality programs to pretty much anything else on the air. Britain's Channel 4 recently produced a series called "1900 House," showcasing a contemporary family living a nineteenth-century life for three months. Yet, interestingly, despite the low-tech formalities one would normally associate with the vicissitudes of Victorian living, the show is strikingly casual in tone. Its narrative unfolds in the manner of the contemporary documentary, with meandering handheld cameras and one-on-one interviews that seem to focus primarily on the inhabitants' frustrations (complaints about compromised heating conditions and the complexity of layered undergarments seem paramount). Indeed, in spite of the graceful, Merchant-Ivoryesque art direction, the show's tone has the impromptu, loosey-goosey feel of an MTV "Spring Break" party. It is freeform and conversational, like a chatroom sprung to life: shards of evocative images, fragments of disconnected conversation, a collage of dislocated moments captured fleetingly on screen. By using real people, the show celebrates averageness and, at the same time, avoids having to be really accurate. The skew here is on the unpredictable foibles of these temporary visitors rather than on the technicalities of life in what now seems, comparatively, a prehistoric phase of the industrial revolution.

"1900 House" is edited with the kind of deliberately messy informality that typifies reality programming in general, and the new illiteracy in particular. Its imperfections make it a quicker, if less accurate, read. Such is the populist reaction to the new world order, one that opposes anything even remotely regulatory: from the demand for design prerequisites to the narrowcasting of intellectual aptitudes to the perseverance of corporate monopolies. In the end, the new illiteracy is our modern-day retaliation against the tyranny of logic. "In this age of raw transcription," writes *The New York Times* columnist William Safire, "art strains to imitate life, and artful writers feel the pressure to mirror the speech patterns of yammering people by imitating their higgledy-piggledy outpouring of unedited thoughts." The promise of personal expression notwithstanding, what ever happened to good editing, smart instincts, and the pursuit of meritocracies? And when, incidentally, did design become the enemy?

One of the more prevalent design conceits to emerge over the course of the last decade is a messy, irreverent kind of Scratchiness, a graphic design take on grunge chic: hand-scrawled and edgy—the antithesis of the hygienic purity of the machine age. Scratchiness is intentionally misaligned and almost purposefully sloppy—a celebration of all that is ill-resolved and non-committal. Like the hand-held camerawork that typified music videos in the mid-80s, it thrives on jumpy cuts and skewed perspectives: it is as if the goal is to do anything but stand still. This essay traces the origins of Scratchiness, from Hans Hoffman's use of the free scrawl to Kyle Cooper's titles for the film *Seven*, and analyzes the tension between formal expression and gestural impermanence.

: Cult of the Scratchy

A decade or more ago, in the spirit of concern for the environment, we began to think deeply about the designer's contribution to global warming and sustainable ecosystems. In simple terms, this meant we started to favor recycled papers, diligently convincing our clients to have their annual reports bound with twigs and string instead of staples and glue. Following the lead begun by our esteemed colleagues in the North Woods of Minnesota, we found ourselves specifying muted colors like Sage and Eglantine, printing on paper with such an aggressive (but pure!) grain you could barely decipher the 6-point type struggling to be read between its crevices. Today, of course, jaded with the 20-20 hindsight that only time and maturity can allow, we look back on this period in design history with a mixture of nostalgia and disdain, equating such aesthetic choices with equally quaint remnants of the past—hanging macramé pots in fern bars, for instance.

Then along came David Carson.

And type started to splinter. And disappear. Things started to bleed where they were not supposed to and images were morphed and muted and ghosted and blurred to abstraction. I will not go into detail here on the particularities of this transitional phase (within which the Carson era historically—albeit somewhat loosely—resides) now known widely as "The Age of the Blur." (Not to be confused with "The Age of Innocence," the Blur Era has already been well-documented by Phil Patton.) In Carson's hands, images were often undecipherable. Ditto the type. Research showed that most of *Beach Culture's* teen-and-twenty-something circulation did not exactly look to the magazine for intellectual enlightenment, so it is likely that Carson was merely doing what the rest of us would have done in his place: finding the form commensurate with the content. Content? Well, anyway. By the time he was knee-deep in *RayGun* we were all subscribing to the magazine, and the readership's demographic target was shot to hell. Here, readability itself came under suspicion and design entered a new phase.

Gone were the twigs and soft sensibilities of yesteryear: in their place, muffled letterforms and mutant type, manipulated imagery, and a kind of compositional frenzy that seemed to challenge the very gravity of the page. Fonts chortled and choked and splintered and spread across spreads and Jan Tschichold did somersaults, poor thing, in his grave. Like anything, this trend took no time to reach that wide berth of cultural mediocrity we all try to ignore, sinking into that abyss between the hopelessly hip and the horrifyingly hokey, that great ever-increasing wasteland of cultural ubiquity. And—sad but true—it was not long before Template Gothic became the font of choice for produce items on the sale rack at Acme.

Then along came Kyle Cooper.

And he. Designed those titles. For. SEVEN the movie that. Well. Those shards of Type shards of Type were. Featured in every design magazine and wonSCREEEEECHevery award and even. Non-designers were talking about it and doing it and COPYING it and somehow, it seemed, the days of Carson were no more. Though to be fair, they might be well considered a stepping stone to this, the new design idiom of the nineties: the Cult of the Scratchy.

Scratchy is everywhere. It is a kind of graphic design take on grunge chic—hand-scrawled type and scratch marks, messy and edgy, the antithesis of the hygienic purity of the machine age. Scratchiness is a kind of celebration of the non-committal. Like the hand-held camera-work that typified music videos in the mid-80s, it thrives on jumpy cuts and skewed perspectives: it is as if the goal is to do anything but stand still. And even though it is largely manifesting itself in screen-based media (from film titles to interface design to TV commercials) leading one to suspect it is itself time-based, Scratchiness is all about simulating movement on a two-dimensional surface.

Consider Peter Girardi's interface design for 1997's *ID Design Review's* interactive winners. It is a masterful orchestration of regener-ated fax art, dots, and squiggles, and a jumpy, fragmented elliptical surface on top of which the content dances and squeaks and slides on by. Or the collateral materials for the Samuel Johnson film, *187:* here the numerals in the title appear to have been scratched onto a plate of glass with a very fine needle, a kind of nails-on-chalkboard interpretation of the classic definition of Scratchiness-as-social irritant. There are numerous, perhaps even countless Websites sporting this new design idiom: from e13.com to eyecandy.com to jodi.org, which one source alleged to be the Mother of all Scratchi-Sites.

Where does it come from, this urge to jiggle and squirm?

In part it is our knee-jerk response to things digital, borne of a fear of projecting the unquestionably static history of our profession onto this new and seemingly kinetic world. So-called "graphic" designers have classically defined themselves, and characterized their profession, through the kinds of behaviors and activities that circumscribed their work: more often than not, these were of a two- (and not three-) dimensional nature. So they consulted type specimen books and made informed decisions about copyfitting and grids and picture placement. Or they developed trademarks, identity systems, and stationery programs. They visualized concepts, but they visualized them flat. Sequence meant turning a page of a book: dramatic impact could be achieved through things like "juxtaposition" and "scale." Through such decidedly two-dimensional impulses graphic designers thus "gestured" to things like sequence, motion, and pace.

But in a world utterly besieged by fast and furious media, the considerations that previously qualified a designer's decision-making no longer seem quite so apt—or applicable. Today, to be in the groove is to be *on the move*. So, like "The Age of the Blur" before it, the popularity of Scratchiness (and its consequent elevation to cult status) may be due, in part, to this indefatigable urge to simulate motion.

There are, of course, innumerable precursors to Scratchiness, not the least of which harkens back to the great (and relatively recent) heyday of xerography and clip art. Its victims included everyone from Charles Spencer Anderson to Tibor Kalman, not to mention the droves of wannabes who followed in their wake. Like "The Cult of the Scratchy," "The Age of the Xerox" was in part prompted by a rejection of slick and sophisticated (think glossy annual reports) in favor of a more simplified yet at the same time more expressive idiom: part nostalgic, part idiosyncratic, it presaged Scratchiness in its aggressive appeal to the erosion of clean form. There was also an economic imperative at work: xeroxing was cheap and clip art was copyright-free, making this a considerably more affordable and efficient way to design. Certainly one would be hard put to imagine similar financial incentives circumscribing today's Scratchers, though a likely explanation can perhaps be found in what appears to be an overwhelming national lust for "designing experience."

"Designing experience," the battle cry of the contemporary designer, can be heard most frequently from those working in new media or attending design school. The degree to which designers liken themselves to film directors is not the fault of the designers themselves so much as a function of the identity crisis they experience at the hands of new (and increasingly kinetic) software programs. It is, of course, enormously seductive to "design" something that not only zooms across the screen as you're designing it, but in addition, comes ready-made with its very own soundtrack.

It has long been my belief that "The Age of The Blur" grew from someone's unintentional screw-up in Photoshop one day, and that the trend itself became a kind of international celebration of a filter. Oddly, for some, there seems to be a direct correlation between software aptitude and fantasies of Hollywood: and alas, no sooner does the aspiring designer learn how to make a Quicktime movie, than he can be found down by the water cooler secretly practicing his Oscar acceptance speech.

What Blur and Scratchy share in common, too, is a kind of design irreverence that is in many ways the antithesis of modernism: here, it is obfuscation—not clarification—that is the goal. It bears saying that there are numerous other stylistic design codes that support and contribute to this notion, from typographic layering to collage, montage, photomontage, and so on—all methods of decomposing and/or reconstructing the surface of something. Such tactics bespeak a level of cultural anxiety that has perhaps found its ideal visual incarnation in the twitchy qualities of Scratchiness. Ironically, too, while such methods may seem at face value to stand out in direct contrast from the principles of certain classic design practitioners—like, for example, Paul Rand—they are not without their historical, and eminently creative, precursors.

Like, for example, Paul Rand.

Wait a minute. How could Rand, a staunch modernist, have had anything to do with this decidedly recent, decidedly anti-modernist design trend? Truth to tell, Scratchiness may be hip but it is not new. More than thirty years ago, essays on metaphysics in art by such notable critics as Harold Rosenberg traced the evolution of space and time, particularly as they related to the creation of a work of art. Rosenberg wrote of what he called "The Aesthetics of Impermanence" and described the Action Painters—Willem de Kooning, Jackson Pollack, Franz Kline, and especially Hans Hoffman, who was one of the first artists to make compositional use of the free scrawl. These early exercises in rhythym, pulse, and the power of the abstract, handmade line were, in a sense, formal explorations of the relationship between passive and active, between push and pull.

Ironically, Rand's famous visual semantics projects—which he assigned for over thirty years at Yale—were based on nearly identical notions of visual tension. In his own work, he incorporated aspects of handwriting and mark-making reminiscent of some of today's more expressive examples of Scratchiness. Was this an early effort to simulate movement on the page? Possibly. Certainly the qualities of playfulness that found their way into Rand's work for over sixty years suggest that there was a very basic connection between mark-making and human expression. And there is little doubt that the importance of the hand in making design lay at the epicenter of his methodology (and craft) for the duration of his life.

So is the "Cult of the Scratchy" all about the introduction—the celebration, even—of the human hand? Is the presence of the human hand representative of the human voice—or more specifically, the designer's voice? Difficult to say, though as a reaction to the frenetic overload of the information age, such interpretive ambiguity is perhaps not all that surprising. And ambiguity is, after all, the great by-product of speed—itself the most prevailing characteristic of our latter-day over-accelerated culture.

"The Cult of the Scratchy" owes its current popularity to a host of influences, some taken broadly (the speed with which information flies through a given day is enough to make anyone afraid to commit to standing still) and some more connected to a specific idea, or person, or expression of fact. Some are internal to the tribe (last week's Carson is this week's Cooper), and some reflect broader, or more classic, or more complex cultural conditions.

There are aspects to Scratchiness that are primitive and childlike, and qualities that gesture to ultra-hip urban sophistication. Trends in design mutate so quickly into one another, it is now becoming eminently possible to comment with great authority on an entire generation of design evolution crammed into about six years: from Twigs to Carson to Blur to Scratchiness. Moreover, it is becoming equally possible to draw conclusions that wrongly classify periods in design history (and the designers who bring them to life), without examining the broader context within which design, like any other fundamentally humanist discipline, can be expected to thrive. In the end, perhaps, if the lessons of modernism have any residual value in this oddly turbulent landscape, then the dictum "form follows function" points us to the most rational conclusion of all: which is to say, there isn't one. If the function is to keep moving, then the form probably will not stick around long enough for any of us to ever really figure it out.

As advances in technology introduce more complex creative challenges, screen-based typography must be reconsidered as a new language with its own grammar, its own syntax, and its own rules. What we need are better models which go beyond language or typography to reinforce—rather than restrict—our understanding of what it is to design with electronic media. This essay traces some of the experimental precursors to contemporary electronic typography—from Marinetti's *Parole in Libertà* to George Maciunas *Fluxxus* happenings—and looks at language as part of a more comprehensive communication platform: time-sensitive, interactive, and highly visual.

: Electronic Typography:
The New Visual Language

In 1968, Mattel introduced Talking Barbie. I like to think of this as my first computer. I remember saving up my allowance for what seemed an eternity to buy one. To make her talk, you pulled a little string; upon its release, slave-to-fashion Barbie would utter delightful little conversational quips like "I think mini-skirts are smashing" and "Let's have a costume party."

If you held the string back slightly as she was talking, her voice would drop a few octaves, transforming her from a chirpy soprano into a slurpy baritone. What came out then sounded a lot more like "Let's have a cocktail party."

I loved that part.

What I loved was playing director—casting her in a new role, assigning her a new (albeit ludicrous) personality. I loved controlling the tone of her voice, altering the rhythm of her words, modulating her oh-so-minimal (and moronic) vocabulary. I loved having the power to shape her language—something I would later investigate typographically, as I struggled to understand the role of the printed word as an emissary of spoken communication.

Today, my Macintosh sounds a lot like my Barbie did then—the same monotone, genderless, robotic drawl. But here in the digital age, the relationship between design and sound—and in particular, between the spoken word and the written word—goes far beyond pulling a string. The truth is that the computer's internal sound capabilities enable us to design with sound, not just in imitation of it. Like it or not, the changes brought about by recent advances in technology indicate the need for designers to broaden their understanding of what it is to work effectively with typography. It is no longer enough to design for readability, to suggest a sentiment or reinforce a concept through the selection of a particular font. Today, we can make type talk: in any language, at any volume, with musical underscoring or sci-fi sound effects or overlapping violins. We can sequence and dissolve, pan and tilt, fade to black, and specify type in sensurround. As we "set" type, we encounter a decision-making process unprecedented in two-dimensional design: unlike the kinetic experience of turning a printed page to sequence information, time now becomes an unusually powerful and persuasive design element.

Today, we can visualize concepts in four action-packed, digital dimensions. Interactive media have introduced a new visual language, one that is no longer bound to traditional definitions of word and image, form and place. Typography, in an environment that offers such diverse riches, must redefine its goals, its purpose, its very identity. It must reinvent itself. And soon.

Visual language, or the interpretation of spoken words through typographic expression, has long been a source of inspiration to artists and writers. Examples abound, dating as far back as the incunabula and extending upwards from concrete poetry in the 1920s to "happenings" in the 1960s to today's multicultural morass of pop culture. Visual wordplay proliferates: from Filippo Tommaso Marinetti's *Parole in Libertà* to George Maciunas' *Fluxxus* installations to the latest MTA posters adorning New York subway walls. Kurt Schwitters, Guillaume Apollinaire, Piet Zwart, Robert Brownjohn—the list is long, the examples inexhaustible.

For designers there has always been an overwhelming interest in formalism, in analyzing the role of type as medium (structure), message (syntax), and muse (sensibility). Throughout, there has been an attempt to reconcile the relationship between words both spoken and seen—a source of exhilaration to some and ennui to others. Lamenting the expressive limitations of the western alphabet, Adolf Loos explained it simply: "One cannot speak a capital letter." Denouncing its structural failings, Stanley Morrison was equally at odds with a tradition that designated hierarchies in the form of upper and lowercase letterforms. Preferring to shape language as he deemed appropriate, Morrison referred to caps as "a necessary evil."

Academic debate over the relationship between language and form has enjoyed renewed popularity in recent years as designers borrow from linguistic models in an attempt to codify—and clarify—their own typographic explorations. Deconstruction's design devotées have eagerly appropriated its terminology and theory, hoping to introduce a new vocabulary for design: it is the vocabulary of signifiers and signifieds, of Jacques Derrida and Ferdinand de Saussure, of Michel Foucault and Umberto Eco.

As a comprehensive model for evaluating typographic expression, deconstruction has ultimately proved both heady and limited. Today, as advances in technology introduce greater and more complex creative challenges, it is simply arcane. We need to look at screen-based typography as a new language, with its own grammar, its own syntax, and its own rules. What we need are new and better models, models that go beyond language or typography *per se*, and that reinforce rather than restrict our understanding of what it is to design with electronic media.

Of course, learning a new language is one thing, fluency quite another. Yet we have come to equate fluency with literacy—another outdated model for evaluation. "Literacy should not mean the ability to decode strings of alphabetic letters," says Seymour Papert, Director of the Epistemology and Learning Group at the MIT Media Lab, who refers to such a definition as "letteracy." And language, even to linguists, proves creatively limiting as a paradigm. "New media promise the opportunity to offer a smoother transition to what really deserves to be called literacy," says Papert. Typography, as the physical embodiment of such thinking, has quite a way to go.

The will to decipher the formal properties of language, a topic of great consequence for communication designers in general, has its philosophical antecedents in ancient Greece. "Spoken words," wrote Aristotle in *Logic*, "are the symbols of mental experience. Written words are the symbols of spoken words." Today, centuries later, the equation has added a new link: what happens when written words can speak? When they can move? When they can be imbued with sound and tone and nuance, with decibel and harmony and voice? As designers probing the creative parameters of this new technology, our goal may be less to digitize than to dramatize. Indeed, there is a theatrical component that I am convinced is essential to this new thinking. Of what value are typographic choices—bold and italics, for example—when words can dance across the screen, dissolve, or disappear altogether?

In this dynamic landscape, our static definitions of typography appear increasingly imperiled. Will the beauty of traditional letterforms be compromised by the evils of this new technology? Will punctuation be stripped of its functional contributions, or ligatures their aesthetic ones? Will type really matter?

Of course it will. In the meantime, however, typography's early appearance on the digital frontier does not bode well for design. Take email, for example. Gone are the days of good handwriting, of the Palmer Method and the penmanship primer. In its place, electronic mail which, despite its futuristic tone, has paradoxically revived the antiquated art of letter writing. Sending email is easy and effortless and quick. It offers a welcome respite from talking, and, consequently, bears a closer stylistic resemblance to conversational speech than to written language. However, for those of us with even the most modest design sense, it eliminates the distinctiveness that typography has traditionally brought to our written communiqués. Though its supporters endorse the democratic nature of such homogeneity, the truth is, it is boring. In the land of email, we all "sound" alike: everyone writes in system fonts.

Email is laden with many such contradictions: ubiquitous in form yet highly diverse in content, at once ephemeral and archival, transmitted in real time yet physically intangible, it is a kind of aesthetic flatland—informationally dense and visually unimaginative. Here, hierarchies are preordained and non-negotiable: passwords, menus, commands, help. Software protocols require that we title our mail, a leftover model from the days of interoffice correspondence, which makes even the most casual letter sound like a corporate memo. As a result, electronic missives all have headlines. (Titling our letters makes us better editors, not better designers.) As a fitting metaphor for the distilled quality of things digital, the focus in email is on the abridged, the acronym, the quick read. Email is functionally serviceable and visually forgettable, not unlike fast food. It is drive-through design: get in, get out, move on.

And it is everywhere. Here is the biggest contribution to communication technology to come out of the last decade, a global network linking millions of people worldwide, and designers—communication designers, no less—are nowhere in sight. Typography, in this envᵢᵣᵤ. ment, desperately needs direction. Where to start? Comparisons with printed matter inevitably fail, as words in the digital domain are processed with a speed unprecedented in the world of paper. Here, they are incorporated into databases or interactive programs, where they are transmitted and accessed in random, non-hierarchical sequences. "Hypertext," or the ability to program text with interactivity—meaning that a word, when clicked upon or pointed to will, in fact, do something—takes it all a step further: here, by introducing alternate paths, information lacks the closure of the traditional printed narrative. "Hypertextual story space is now multidimensional," explains Robert Coover in the magazine *Artforum*, "and theoretically infinite."

If graphic design can be largely characterized by its attention to understanding the hierarchy of information (and using type in accordance with such understanding), then how are we to determine its use in a nonlinear context such as this? On a purely visual level, we are limited by what the pixel will render: the screen matrix simulates curves with surprising sophistication, but hairlines and serifs will, to the serious typophile, appear inevitably compromised. On a more objective level, type in this context is both silent and static, and must compete with sound and motion—not an easy task. Conversely, in the era of the handheld television remote, where the user can—and does—mute at will, the visual impact of written typography is not to be discounted.

To better analyze the role(s) of electronic typography, we might begin by looking outside: not to remote classifications imported from linguistic textbooks, or even to traditional design theories conveniently repackaged, but to our own innate intelligence and distinctive powers of creative thought. To cultivate and adequately develop this new typography (because if we don't, no one else will), we might do well to rethink visual language altogether, to consider new and alternative perspectives. "If language is indeed the limit of our world," writes literary critic William Gass in *Habitations of the Word*, "then we must find another, larger, stronger, more inventive language which will burst those limits."

In his book *Seeing Voices*, author and neurologist Oliver Sacks reflects on the complexity of sign language, and describes the cognitive understanding of spatial grammar in a language that exists without sound. He cites the example of a deaf child learning to sign, and details the remarkable quality of her visual awareness and descriptive, spatial capabilities. "By the age of four, indeed, Charlotte had advanced so far into visual thinking and language that she was able to provide new ways of thinking—revelations—to her parents." As a consequence of learning sign language as adults, this particular child's parents not only learned a new language, but discovered new ways of thinking as well—visual thinking. Imagine the potential for interactive media if designers were to approach electronic typography with this kind of ingenuity and openmindedness.

William Stokoe, a Chaucer scholar who taught Shakespeare at Gallaudet College in the 1950s, summarized it this way: "In a signed language, narrative is no longer linear and prosaic. Instead, the essence of sign language is to cut from a normal view to a close-up to a distant shot to a close-up again, and so on, even including flashback and fast-forward scenes, exactly as a movie editor works." Here, perhaps, is another model for visual thinking: a new way of shaping meaning based on multiple points of view, which sees language as part of a more comprehensive communication platform—time-sensitive, interactive, and highly visual. Much like multimedia.

In bringing the Big Reveal to the little screen, the typographic rollover has galvanized our expectations of classic story structure, and in so doing, has introduced new and radical theatrical considerations to the way we think about shaping graphic evidence in time-based media. In this context, the consequences for moveable, mutable, morphable type are considerable. This essay looks at new cognitive layers of suggestion, increased meaning, and a new kind of theatrical typography that is revolutionizing the visual display of complex narratives.

: The Big Reveal and the Dance of the Mouse

In the mid-1980s, I worked for eighteen months as a daytime television script writer. During this unusually protracted lapse in my design career (to say nothing of the questionable lapse in judgment, let alone taste) I wrote long-term story projections (called "bibles"), script outlines ("breakdowns") and I wrote scripts, which meant I wrote dialogue I would slave over, hoping to mimic the rhythm of the way a certain actor spoke, looking to reinforce indelible character traits through the cadences of my graceful prose. The actors received their scripts a day or so before shooting, paraphrasing said prose with an irritating disinterest—a humbling process in and of itself. And a collaborative one: Once a week, I gathered with nine other staff writers for a story meeting where we debated logistics. How to deal with an off-screen pregnancy (emphasize facial close-ups and shoot above the neck); how to deal with a character who in real life had asked for a raise (kill him off); or who needed four months off to shoot a movie (kill him off, then introduce his identical, though deranged, twin brother—lo and behold—four months later); how to deal with forty contract players who would get paid whether you used them or not (build in a party scene, time-pegged to anything even marginally celebratory—the discovery of Antarctica, for instance.) Health emergencies and courtroom dramas were written with the support of telephone hotlines providing access to medical specialists and legal experts. I once spent an hour on the phone consulting with a Canadian cardiologist on the proper descriptive language for victims of electrical shock. (The character in question, seeking emergency shelter during—what else?—a tornado, had opened a screen door by grabbing its metal handle.) It was under these somewhat rarified circumstances that I was thus able to write with surprising authority about defibrillators and demonic worship, crash carts and custody battles, triage, extortion, and the vicissitudes of infidelity.

Though in the end I found it increasingly difficult to take any of it seriously, there were aspects of my life as a daytime television writer that I rather enjoyed. I once wrote a dynamically sequenced suicide scene, in which the narrative unfolded in a rapidly intercut crescendo between a sentimental church wedding and a spurned lover's majestic leap off a city bridge. Would she or wouldn't she survive? (She did, though in true serial style, the episode aired on Christmas Eve, hooking viewers over an extended holiday weekend.) Seizing creative license where I could find it, I delighted in writing in casual references to my friends and enemies: I soon became quite adept at naming villains after fascist dictators, war criminals, and the occasional ex-boyfriend. Defying the moronic nature of certain pointless scenes, I frequently found myself scripting absurd moments of kinetic hyperactivity. I remember a scene in which a young ingenue (played by a then-unknown comic actress named Meg Ryan) struggled with a piece of toast caught in a toaster as she delivered her now eminently forget-table lines. On television and in the theatre, this kind of vaudevillian activity is known as "business": it is a kind of physical choreography that provides a visual counterpoint to the unfolding verbal narrative. (As I dimly recall, the toaster dance was intended at once to distract Ryan's on-screen husband and conceal her on-screen lover hiding in the closet.) Business is used to amuse the audience, to illuminate a character detail, or to physically communicate some aspect of the plot that would otherwise require a kind of expository dialogue: dialogue that telegraphs the ending, overstates the obvious, or reveals too much too soon. Indeed, the precision required to stage such revelation—quite literally, phasing the tension between establishing conflict and orches-trating its cresecendo, denouement and eventual resolution—is a critical dramatic tool, and relies on nothing less than impeccable timing. We called it "The Big Reveal."

I offer my own experience as a television writer as a preamble here because the methodologies in design are perhaps not so dissim-ilar: like writers, designers (particularly those engaged in new media) wrestle with issues of orchestration, presentation, and articulation, and struggle to identify their exposition over time. In televised drama, like in theatre and film, a story's underlying armature relies upon certain fundamental narrative tools: the classic Hollywood three-act paradigm, from which most television shows are loosely adapted, provides a solid, if somewhat formulaic structure intended to guide the dramatic action forward. Whether or not we possess similar editorial models to shape dramatic and visual orchestrations on the Web remains another question entirely, though on many contemporary "dynamic" Websites, there is perhaps a parallel organizational structure at play: these sites now open with fairly ambitious film shorts (formerly called "splash" pages) which, like film trailers, introduce the tone and spirit of the site about to be revealed. Unlike film, however, such opening animations are largely intended to disguise—rather than reveal—the "loading" of their parent sites. These somewhat elaborate mini-movies are Web variants of basic theatrical business: simply stated, they are little more than brief (and occasionally burlesque) digital adaptations of the age-old drama of distraction.

And the similarities hardly end there. Typographic choices on a site, like actors on TV, frequently become our primary emissaries of communication: they are all about posture and characterization. (On this topic, the American satirist H. L. Mencken once wrote that there should be a typeface that slants backwards, for irony.) Now here is where it gets really interesting. If a designer once made typographic choices that embraced a wide yet essentially static set of conditions, these were decisions that could be counted on to virtually insure a kind of dependable consistency. Type in books, for instance, intentionally evokes a set of formal conditions that allow the content to be both well-supported and reliably cohesive. But unlike book typography, this new screen typography dances; it sings; it shouts; it does somersaults and cartwheels, and *then,* when it settles down, just as you think you have got a hold on it, you mouse over a word and it transforms instantly into something completely different.

It is the Big Reveal, and it is perhaps the most stunning change in typographic form-giving since the invention of moveable type. In this medium, type is no longer an empty vessel, silently poised at the perimeter of a page—form awaiting content. This new theatrical typography *is* content, revealing its subtext, reinforcing its context, captivating and catapulting the viewer toward new cognitive layers of suggestion, increased meaning and added depth. What is more, this new typography only comes to life when a person touches a mouse and rolls over a word. (The relative subtlety here is astonishing: the word is not even clicked upon—it is *rolled* upon.)

In a fascinating perceptual reversal from the early days of the New Economy, which didactically proclaimed the Cartesian virtues of user-selected empowerment ("I click therefore I am"), rollovers are mysterious and hidden, like secret land mines. They are elusive: you quickly find yourself poking about the screen for hints of their presence, pursuing them madly like an obsessed lover. They are playful: you recoil when they surprise you, yet are quickly reminded that they can be programmed randomly to provoke a different response mechanism each time they are activated. And they are oddly, yet deliriously choreographic: rollovers engage us in an enchanting *pas-de-deux* between the screen and the mouse, the hand and the eye, the reader, the word and the idea. What soon becomes clear is that the Big Reveal is not enabled by a click-through on a navigation bar. It is not made possible by a bunch of union-approved writers plotting a story and constructing its careful evolution over time. It is activated by your hand, rolling over a series of letterforms, transforming a word into an idea into a translation into an argument into a counter-argument into a mathematical equation into a Shakespearean sonnet. It is like giving language (and by association, typography) its own self-actualizing oxygen supply. And the effect is nothing less than magical.

Of course, you can roll over an image, or a pattern, or a grid just as easily as you can roll over a word: the rollover itself can be applied to anything on the screen. But when it is language that is being transformed—and in design terms, this means deploying typographic nuances to mediate that transformation—there is perhaps something more unusual taking place. First, it suggests a new idiomatic use for typography: let's call it choreo-typography, because it relies as much upon kinetic orchestrations as stylistic conceits. Next, there is the question of timing: how can the order of things rolled upon (and yes, eventually clicked upon) impact upon the "reading" of a story by challenging its classic linear progression? (Websites often rely upon axial structures—horizontal and/or vertical navigation bars, for instance—to guide a user's progression. Such logic is obviously challenged, if not thwarted entirely by the idiosyncratic and somewhat parenthetical messages liberated by the meandering rollover.) Finally and most importantly, typography can now be endowed with dramatic qualities, among them, subtext (what is really happening beneath the surface?) and context (how might that surface be extrapolated and extended across a site or story?).

In bringing the Big Reveal to the little screen, the typographic rollover has galvanized our expectations of classic story structure, and in so doing, has introduced new and radical theatrical considerations to the way we think about shaping graphic evidence in time-based media. In this context, the consequences for moveable, mutable, morphable type are considerable.

The idea that revelation, in narrative terms, can be made evident through means at once physical (you move the cursor) and visual (you uncover something new) is what is really Big. Yet beyond the subtle typographic pratfalls beginning to surface on certain experimental sites, few have yet to truly engage the typographic opportunities (let alone the opportunities for an entirely unprecedented form of graphic authorship) liberated by the rollover's dramatic potential: letterforms dissolving, words exploding, storylines unravelling—where will it all lead? Taken to its extreme, if logical, conclusion, isn't the act of "revealing" something merely a slow, gradual process of elimination? (This is the working metaphor behind such successful TV programs as "Survivor," "Big Brother," and the recent hit "The Weakest Link," in which participants seek, quite literally, to "reveal" fatal flaws that result in eradicating their opponents live—and on screen. It is a grim and somewhat menacing notion: rollover as annihilator.)

Perhaps the best model is a theatrical one: and indeed, while the perceptual shifts made possible by rollovers may imply a chameleon-like role for screen typography, quite the opposite may, in fact, be true. In his classic paradox of acting, the French theorist Diderot wrote a century ago that in order to move the audience the actor must himself remain unmoved. Now imagine the comparative role for type on the screen. Unmoved, yes: type remains true to its own noble heritage, and good kerning prevails. But unmoving? Not a chance.

As we struggle to reconcile our conflicting reactions to information overload, the dramatic (and dynamic) model of filmic storytelling offers a more compelling way to think about the power of visual narrative. From scene to sequence, montage to *mise-en-scène*, visual staging on the screen has a long, distinguished history. Yet it would seem that this rich legacy has been virtually ignored in the design and development of interactive, screen-based media. This essay examines the critical relationship between storytelling and visual representation in a dynamic environment characterized by networked exchange—and perpetual interruption.

: New Media, New Narrative: The Lost Legacy of Film

Over dinner recently, my mother recounted a passage from *The Alexandria Quartet*. Although her most recent reading had been years ago, her face lit up as she cited certain key moments—the names of characters, descriptions of settings, meaningful fragments of her own reading of this text. Her detailed recollections were delivered with enthusiasm and delight, a testament to the evocative durability of Lawrence Durrell's epic tale.

It occurred to me that I had never heard anyone describe an experience with interactive media in quite the same way. This book had meant something to my mother: one might even say that her reading of it had been interactive. Even had Durrell not structured the four volumes of the *Quartet* to be read in any order—an early, and by contemporary standards, crude, experiment in interactivity—I suspect she would have derived the same pleasure from his novels. My mother's references were personal, idiosyncratic; her interpretations specific to her own life experience. By choosing to read the story again years later, she had further enriched her experience of its narrative, its characters and setting, its unusual dimensions.

One of the great gifts of fiction lies in its ability to do precisely this: to transport us to a different time and place, an alternative space in which we make silent observations, imperceptibly casting ourselves inside a story's domain. We often experience a trip to the movies in a similar way. Captive in a darkened room, the immense scale of the screen exorcises any dueling reality, leaving our focus streamlined and our attention riveted. Does this kind of mesmerizing interaction demand total darkness to fully enlist our attention? Or can interactive technologies—and their designers—hope to achieve a similar goal?

"Interactivity" with the screen has been, up until very recently, primarily a consequence of seeing and responding internally—viscerally, even—to a moment observed. For over a century it has remained the role of the writer, the director, and cinematographer (and on occasion, the designer) to render a moment in time through plot and character, sound, motion, and emotion. Over time, as technology grew to support greater complexity in film-*making*, so, too, did the variety of our reactions to the screen: pain and laughter, fear, terror, anticipation and excitement. The public's continued love affair with the movies is a constant reminder of the enduring power of the screen as an engaging, seductive, even hypnotic medium.

As we struggle to reconcile our conflicting reactions to information overload, the dramatic—and dynamic—model of filmic storytelling offers a more compelling way to think about the power of visual narrative. From scene to sequence, montage to *mise-en-scène*, visual staging on the screen has a long and distinguished history. Why has this rich legacy been virtually ignored in the design and development of interactive screen-based media?

Over the last decade, the growth of the consumer electronics market has introduced opportunities for designers ranging from on-air graphics to video games to a host of information services, requiring a skill that has come to be commonly referred to as interface design. Led (and occasionally restricted) by the technology that serves us, its visual vocabulary has emerged as a reductive pictorial syntax, an ironic casualty of late twentieth-century modernism taken to an info-graphic extreme. Efforts to make complex information accessible to all have resulted in a new global language of sterile, stilted iconography: miniature hieroglyphs featuring cartoon-like facsimiles of task-driven processes, file folders and trashcans, and, most recently (and lamentably), emoticons. In earlier essays I have discussed what critic Andrew Olds dubbed an "ideogrammatic mode of organization," expressing my own dissatisfaction with what I have come to refer to as the desktop legacy: the icon-driven graphical language that is, to date, the dubious aesthetic hallmark of the so-called computer age.

Today, these intransigent emblems of consumer technology offer little leeway for expressing the greater complexities introduced by dynamic, time-based media. Better to look at the narrative models suggested by screens other than the computer: most notably, the silver one.

For the better part of this century, the designer's contribution to film has resided largely in the creation of title sequences. Like the shaping of information on a package or book jacket, titles are critical to our immediate perception of the underlying content. They bespeak, in a sense, the film's corporate identity: uniting form and content, they are uniquely and critically connected to our immediate responses, responses reflected in box office receipts and Oscar nominations and, ultimately, the economic livelihood of the movie industry as a whole.

Yet even given some of the more inspired examples often cited in the design press, film titles dwell at the physical peripheries of the movies themselves. Ultimately, their role *lies* somewhere between the promotional and the propagandistic. Their principal duty is to introduce functional information rooted in contractual imperatives: billing and credits are serious business, particularly if you are the star and your agreement stipulates that your name precede the title of the film itself. (In this view, the design challenge becomes a strategic mediation between storytelling and story *selling*.)

This is not to minimize the impact that titles can and should have on a film's identity and the introduction of its narrative. Like the rigors evident in any other design process, good film title design reflects a significant understanding of content, and a clear ability to visualize that content into a dynamic form at once suitable and surprising. There is a choreographic component to all of this that demands an attention to the relationship between visual and aural stimuli, matching representative sequences to cuts from the film's soundtrack, for instance.

Still, the design of titles remains a highly controlled process. Yet more and more, as we enter a world in which the dissemination of information is controlled by a new and increasingly eclectic generation of viewers, the kind of thinking that once drove such one-way design decisions must be remodeled. With interaction comes choice, followed invariably by chaos—unless "good design" intervenes in the form of navigational support.

Actually, that is not true. Interaction design is not only information design: it demands, instead, more comprehensive thinking that involves cognitive, spatial, and ergonomic considerations. As richer, more complex content finds its way into the electronic sphere, the design challenges for shaping that content demand more than mere attention to directional clarity. Like the filmic model cited earlier, successful visual communication will become critically dependent upon our understanding of narrative, of audience, and of drama.

The classic Aristotelian definition of narrative is a story that has a beginning, a middle, and an end. The traditional structuralist definition suggests that this breaks down to a two-tiered model of "story" and "discourse." In a contemporary variant on this view that may be more relevant to interaction design, critic Hamett Nurosi posits "the presentation of an event or a sequence of events that are connected by subject matter and related by time and space." His own bifurcated analysis suggests a deconstruction of narrative that subdivides "story" from "storyteller." The early twentieth-century novelist D. H. Lawrence held a more skeptical view. "Trust the tale," he wrote, "not the teller."

What happens when the story, by virtue of its distribution in a digital environment, becomes infinitely changeable? In time-based media, we no longer have control over hierarchical relationships. Communication is no longer rhetorical. Stories do not necessarily have a beginning, middle, and an end. How do we design for such perpetual and unpredictable interruption? If each viewer becomes the *de facto* storyteller, how do we maintain the integrity of authorship, the focus of plot, the lyrical cadences of a storyteller's voice and vision and point-of-view? As interactive technologies grow more complex, we are witnessing the emergence of a kind of shared authorship in which the linear parameters of classic narrative structure may no longer apply.

If, as designers, we are asked to consider the permutations of a story, our role typically has involved articulating the formal ways in which the story is rendered visually manifest. We think in terms of point and counterpoint, word and image, pacing and sequencing, cropping and juxtaposing. In this medium, however, we must devise new methods for visualizing stories in multiple layers, for designing with multiple points of entry.

One of these layers, of course, is visual. Another is textual. Another is informational. Still another is dramatic. There are time and motion and sound to be considered, and finally, there is "hypertext"—the ability to link ideas and images—which redefines the message transmitted by virtue of its connection to the message received.

The interpretive flexibility inherent in such new media suggests that point of view is itself a powerful narrative tool. Consider Akiro Kurosawa's 1951 film, *Rashomon*. Here, the spine of the story bases itself on a single crime that has been committed. The story is then told through the "viewpoints" of various characters. At once a rich tapestry of multiple perceptions, our attention is equally riveted by the telling of each individual story: multiple points of entry with a singular plot-line. Each character in the film is an eyewitness: so, too, are we.

The concept of the eyewitness is central to thinking about the new visual narrative. It places the emphasis on the viewer, the end-user, the beholder of that information. It values the power of individual observation over the one-sidedness of oration, and, in so doing, makes the experience of viewing that much more memorable. It challenges traditional expectations of form and content, of author and audience, perhaps even of beginnings and endings. The audience, central to this interaction, is the protagonist.

The challenge to the designer, then, is to mediate this interaction. Film director Sergei Eisenstein, who was trained as an engineer and an architect, described his role as a visual storyteller as a "contra-puntal method combining visual and aural images." His objective was to reduce complexity to a "common denominator" on behalf of what he considered to be a singular audience. Though perhaps no longer applicable in today's multimedia market, Eisenstein's goal of repre-senting the intricacies of human experience through a carefully articulated armature of audiovisual phenomena remains a timeless model for study.

With today's interactive products comes a new definition of audi-ence: no longer passive, theirs is a new kind of authority, offering enhanced choice as well as enhanced participation. This emphasis on participation may be the most compelling aspect of interactive tech-nology, yet it jeopardizes our classic notions of the linear presentation of narrative form. Will such participation breed chaos, or even contempt?

Such random, wanton "choice" may not, in the end, be a necessary incentive to viewer interest. The screen is, and has always been, an immersive medium: in the movies our participation with it may be passive in a physical sense, but our attention—visually, psychologi-cally—is riveted because of its evocative capacity to draw us in. This remains one of the most enduring legacies of film, and one that today's interaction "screen" designers would be well advised to consider.

The relationship between what we see, what we hear and what is ultimately recorded by the mind is of enormous consequence today, as the invasion of sound—pagers and beepers, car alarms and cell phones, TV and radio and the Web—extend the media spectrum by raising and distorting our perceptual (read visual) expectations. This essay looks at the encroachment of sound in screen-based media and questions its impact on our appreciation of—and contribution to—the evolution of visual phenomena. In a world gone virtual, if you cannot hear it, is it really there? Are you really there?

: On Sound, Authenticity, and Cultural Amnesia

Among the 75,000 French Jews deported during the Second World War were more than 11,000 children of whom it is estimated a mere 300 survived. In his astonishing book *French Children of the Holocaust,* the author and noted Nazi hunter Serge Klarsfeld (best known as the attorney who brought Klaus Barbie to justice) has meticulously documented the abbreviated biographies of each child, unearthing some 2,500 of their photographs along the way. The language of this book is simple, the details excruciatingly accurate: names, ages, addresses, deportation details, convoy numbers. Collectively, the photographs themselves—most modest family snapshots that reveal nothing of the unthinkable tragedies to come—are a direct visual response to what Jacques Derrida once termed "the traces of being … still calling within the silence of cultural amnesia." Referencing his writings in particular as he gestures to the broader implications of the Holocaust, Derrida writes: "How can these silent voices be made audible within (the text) … which is destined for the eye?"

The relationship between what we see, what we hear and what is ultimately recorded by the mind is of enormous consequence today, as the invasion of sound—pagers and beepers, car alarms and cell phones, TV and radio and the Web (collectively representing the "real-audio"-ization of the free world)—extend the media spectrum by raising and distorting our perceptual (read visual) expectations. "Adaptable to a fault," writes cultural critic Mark Slouka in a recent issue of *Harpers,* "we embrace this brave new cacaphony, attuned, like apprentice ornithologists, to the distinguishing calls of a mechanical phylum."

Silence, in contemporary life, is not only a commodity, it is an endangered species: hard to come by, harder still to sustain, and oddly associated with a kind of anachronistic world view: silence is the stuff of old media, a body of stillness, an inert mass. In today's 24x7 multiplex of sensory input, we have come to identify (and accept) what Slouka calls this "auditory landscape" as a new lexicon, a built-in yet discordant soundtrack of accidental sound bytes juxtaposed against—and superimposed upon—the already noisy world we inhabit.

Evidently, the implications for design are considerable: it is no longer enough to design something merely by making visual choices. A poster is viewed from a passing vehicle: it becomes the visual counterpoint to the flow of traffic, a two-dimensional blip on the kinetic landscape. A text is seldom a text, but more likely a compendium of visual, verbal, and aural clues—an image here, its accompanying soundtrack there, click here to search for "more like this." Cue the siren blaring, the baby crying, the overture from *Schindler's List:* would looking at Klarsfeld's book with such additional audio input augment our ability to feel, to understand—to remember?

Remarkably, quite the opposite is true. Stripped of our loud and imposing modern references, this book is refreshingly media-free. And it is this, this silence—both real and imagined—that is most indelible, most gripping, and most unforgettable.

Not long ago, I came upon an excerpt from a diary, written by a journalist in Belgrade, Jasmina Tesanovic, documenting the disorientation of her life for two weeks during the Balkan war in April 1999. No pictures, no sound, no design details—just words, typeset in the visually anonymous system-font of the Internet, which is where she posted her diary. She writes:

During the day we live the Serbian war: new identity cards, walk on bridges, solidarity among hurt people ... During the night we have the NATO war: detonations, fires, shelters ... Yesterday a journalist was killed in the center of Belgrade, in front of his house, in the middle of the day. Is this war too, and whose war is this now? Who's next?

War is perhaps an extreme set of conditions within which to frame an argument for (or against) the precarious relationship between sound and design. But it is also a contemporary and very real set of conditions. Death, destruction, and displacement. The abolishment of personal property—marriage certificates, birth certificates—that destroys the printed evidence of a person's life, eradicates their history, eliminates their memory.

In the context of war—of totalitarian rule and humanitarian struggle—it is perhaps easy to equate silence with repression and censorship, with fascism and control. Sound, in this context, represents the voice of the individual and introduces a kind of renewed personal (and political) activism: not just hearing but being heard.

Is what we hear more enduring than what we see?

It is the absence of sound, in the pursuit of a deeper or more lasting meaning, that is perhaps of particular interest. Klarsfeld calls his book "an instrument of memory." But what is it, exactly, that we have remembered? Today, as we witness the kind of cultural amnesia that leaves 600,000 ethnic Albanians homeless, the atrocities of war remain dutifully transmitted to us daily via satellite feeds, video footage, news briefings: pictures and words together, each complementing the other, borne of the essential components of the designer's core vocabulary. (Technology cannot save those lost birth certificates, but it does keep us informed.) Along comes sound: does hearing a building blowing up boost our visual interest, our visceral attention, our willingness to believe?

It is a kind of *Star Wars* take on modern technology: Sound invades our orbit, surrounds our senses, and wakes us up. It dictates just what it is we are supposed to feel. It takes over. It seduces. But does it add to our capacity to remember? And given such complex orchestrations in the sensory delivery of information—does design?

Maybe this is what bothers me: the use of sound, as a component in the visualization of ideas, represents a fundamental corruption to the senses. It telegraphs the ending. It prevents the mind from completing the gesture. It interrupts interpretation. It brainwashes the audience. And, more often than not, it drives the design, so that visual matter is, in a sense, choreographed to mimic the ebb and flow of the music, to respond to changes in rhythm, to mirror a voiceover, a crescendo, a bridge, or a refrain. Sound makes design feel gratuitous, decorative, superfluous. Design becomes secondary. Sound rules.

A film professor I know sends his students out each year on their first assignment and asks them to shoot without sound. "Sound lies," he maintains, stressing the dominance of aural stimuli—voices, music, noise, sound effects—over visual phenomena. He is, of course, completely right. Filming in silence, one is immediately made aware of the physical details—the lighting, pacing, depth of field, facial characterstics—that collectively bespeak a visual narrative. Add the audio and boom: you are hooked. In the context of watching something, the encroachment of sound, that most seductive of mood-enhancers, simply takes over.

Today, my students all want to design with sound. They want design to dance and hop and skip, conveying instant attitude, free drama. They want soundtracks and underscoring to accompany their work, as if lending a more dynamic credibility—percussive, sensuous, even goofy—to the visual choices they make makes them more credible choices.

If design was once sound-free—you looked at a poster and were responsible for your own conceptual associations—does the introduction of sound now add to the perceived value of something designed, enhancing its capacity to reach and engage an audience? What is troubling, perhaps, is the degree to which audiences have come not only to expect the audio accompaniment but, at the same time, to expect full production values—what Cole Porter, lyricizing over forty-five years ago on the then-tantalizing thrills of motion pictures, called, in one breath, "breathtaking-cinemascope-and-stereophonic-sound." Today we see-hear-experience it unwittingly through a perpetual influx of aberrantly ambient noises that pierce and penetrate our daily odysseys: we have come to both anticipate and accept the beeps and bells, the alarms and alerts, the synthetic sounds that accompany an innocent trip to the supermarket or the temporary incarceration of an elevator ride. The audio byte has become its own theme song, a pervasive and inescapable cultural phenomenon whose ubiquitous presence in all aspects of our lives—design among them—reflects an almost global preoccupation with sound as a kind of validating force. In a world gone virtual, if you cannot hear it, is it really there? Are you really there?

Though it is unlikely that in and of itself, design will ever be capable of saving the world, eliminating hunger, or restoring peace to embattled nations, the degree to which it can be used to facilitate exchange, disseminate ideas, and elucidate information remains central to its essential value. That said, the fact that May 7th–8th 1999 (overnight), NATO forces erroneously bombed the Chinese embassy in Belgrade—misdirected, as it turns out, because they were referring to long outdated maps—suggests that information design gone awry can prove lethal. (One can only imagine the glee this argument will bring to those advocating the death of print.)

Meanwhile, I long for silence, for a more thoughtfully managed set of media codes in my life. I love music. I watch—and listen to—TV. And

I enjoy, in spite of myself sometimes, the oddly disorienting sensory juxtapositions of the car radio: how differently one can be made to feel driving through the countryside listening to Debussy one minute, Dylan the next. That kind of "user-driven" sound (and this is clearly the great appeal of portable and personalizeable technologies) invites the user to choose the sound input and to consciously pair it with other sensory experience. Conversely, it is the forced connection between design and sound that robs me of that choice, much as it may empower its designer, its author, or its composer.

There are, perhaps, more provocative ways for visual thinkers to contribute to this contemporary media landscape, a new way of embracing sound which includes the absence of sound, a variant, if you will, on information architecture: musical architecture, a phrase coined by the late John Cage. "Musical architecture," Cage once wrote, "produces a new sense of location for thinking and becomes a different place that was always in the air for someone to notice … like silence."

Klarsfeld's book will make you cry. You do not need a soundtrack of plaintive violin solos, or the re-enactment of rumbling trucks over cobblestones, or anything other than your own mind and heart to imagine what it must have felt like to be one of those children, your life extinguished, your destiny denied. Look at this book. Remember it. The silence is deafening.

The images we remember are those that stop time. And in so doing, they co-opt our senses and captivate our attention. Images themselves—at least the kind we remember—tend to be layered and complex, often contradictory, seldom explainable. They haunt and delight us, inspire us, revile us, and possess the somewhat mysterious capacity to become almost obsessively real: pictures provoke us by challenging our perception of (and hunger for) visual authenticity. This essay looks at the mesmerizing value of the still image against the cultural backdrop of multimedia, demonstrating that ironically and in spite of the increasing emphasis we place on pictures that move, the images we tend to recall, quite often, are those that stand perfectly still.

My neighbor, Laura, is twenty-two years old and she is a widow. She leads a quiet life, her activities framed by the routine, custodial duties of single parenthood. But last summer, a trampoline suddenly appeared in her garden. For weeks it sat idly like a wayward shrub, an elasticized disk awkwardly perched on narrow, aluminum legs.

And then, driving by one evening at dusk, I saw Laura flying through the air.

Jumping with her babies, the trampoline at their feet, it was a mesmerizing sight: this young woman—almost a child herself—leaping majestically, defying the odds of gravity, the odds, it seemed, of life. And though they were in constant motion as I drove by, what I remember is just this: three graceful figures suspended in animation, frozen in time. And, to this day, in my memory.

The relationship between human memory and the tenacity of images cannot be underestimated. The actual formation of the image (what Eisenstein called the "mechanics" of the image) is itself a fascinating and largely unpredictable process, made up of associations and expectations, feelings and observations, reactions, sensations, reverberations in the mind and in the memory. An image is both initially perceived and later remembered as a consequence of this somewhat delicate psychological choreography. (The image of the trampoline itself has no value: understood in the context of my neighbor's unusual life, it acquires meaning.)

The remembered image is archived like a microchip in the psyche—the visual equivalent of a sound byte. It is a collapsed montage, reconstructed by the mind into a more temporally efficient, spatially comprehensible and emotionally resonant form. What remains is a kind of improvised 2D sensory snapshot that not only collapses time and space, but also distills meaning, movement, and memory. We "see" the single, representative image in our mind's eye, but in reality it bespeaks a more layered set of conditions, a more complex set of experiences, and an entire host of representations derived from a broader and richer context. Ironically, and in spite of the increasing emphasis we place on pictures that move, the images we tend to recall, quite often, are those that stand perfectly still.

In its purest, most literal incarnation, the image offers documentary, almost diagnostic proof of something. For more than forty years, the legendary American designer Charles Eames photographed his work in microscopic detail, believing that the resulting images would reveal critical information, a visual record that could be fed back into his ongoing working process. Conversely, the Austrian architect Adolf Loos deliberately destroyed his archives, abolishing all two-dimensional traces of his own equally prolific output. For Eames, the image was a tool; for Loos it was a trap. Eames believed images gave renewed meaning to his work, while Loos distrusted the way photographs flattened architectural space, compromising its most valuable—and intangible—assets: light, shadow, dimensionality, and, most importantly, time.

Perhaps more than anything, time affects the way we access, digest, and respond to an image. It is easy to believe that time-based media yield more information because they are moving faster and packing more in—while conversely, the opposite is more likely to be true. "Image stasis promotes data output," observes photography critic Max Kozloff. "And who would deny that (the) pictures themselves are equipped to furnish such factual dividends by virtue of their mechanical ability to stop time?"

The images we remember are those that do indeed stop time. And in so doing, they co-opt our senses and captivate our attention. Images themselves—at least the kind we remember—tend to be layered and complex, often contradictory, seldom explainable. They haunt and delight us, inspire us, revile us, and possess the somewhat mysterious capacity to become almost obsessively real: pictures provoke us by challenging our perception of—and hunger for—visual authenticity.

How else to explain the hypnotic lure of movies projected on screen, the addiction of episodic television, the drama of magnified pseudo-porn on Calvin Klein billboards, the strategically coercive practice of picture-driven selling that promotes the kinds of images that quite literally implant themselves on our brains? Of this madness, Isaac Bashevis Singer once wrote: "You get something in your head and you cannot drive it away."

And so it is with images. There are images that win Pulitzer Prizes and images that sell shampoo. There are images that make us tremble and images that make us laugh. There are narrative images that inform; entertaining images that delight; contradictory images that give us pause, compelling images that make us think. Designers do not generally make images so much as aggregate them: we give critical editorial consideration to their selection, to their relative scale and position, to the way they are framed and situated and composed. And because we participate in various aspects of their manufacture, we contribute—whether implicitly or explicitly, consciously or unconsciously—to their seemingly endless consumption. Caught between the spirit of acceleration that typifies contemporary culture (make it fast!) and the economy of means that has come to characterize all things modern (keep it simple!) designers strive to create imagery that is pithy, arresting, and for lack of a better term—new.

Pity that the shock of the new is, well, anything but new.

At turns shocking, surreal, or suggestive, the effects generated by advertising, television, and online venues suggest that images sell better when they surprise us. But does this make them better, or more authentic, or, quite frankly—more memorable? Invariably, we remain intrigued by the effort taken to twist graphic evidence, to invert—or divert—our sensory preconceptions. "The attempt to make things new through quirkiness," argues critic Henry Allen, "can have an effect both comic and disquieting."

Consider the following and ask yourself: is such gestural manipulation the best way to make us remember? Is it the only way to remember?

SHOCKING IMAGES: *Just Get Hurt*
Sometimes our attention is pulled not so much by the static image as by its displacement: this is as much a design conceit as an editorial decision. Such is the case in the recent Wieden and Kennedy Nike campaign, "Beautiful," which features injured and maimed athletes—a "can you top this?" exaggeration of their award-winning "Just Do It" series. The resonant image is of the athlete—the toothless hockey player, the blind rodeo cowboy—who gave it all, sacrificing the body (but not, it should be noted, the footwear) in the process. *Newsweek's* Adam Bryant questioned the agency's motives, going to extreme

lengths to "cut through the clutter" in a competitive market. Bryant writes: "The Nike (campaign) is a compelling example of what it takes to get people's attention in an age when multitasking is a way of life." Such attention-getting imagery recalls the profile on Death Row inmates featured in a recent issue of Benetton's *Colors*. Like *Colors*, too, Nike rejects the gleeful optimism associated with classic salesmanship practice and succeeds in its anti-branding of the brand. It is coquettishly subversive—and intentionally so. And it will probably sell a lot of shoes.

SURREAL IMAGES: *Celebrating Subtext*

Imagery that disturbs us and jolts our senses may cut through the clutter, but it is slapstick: it is a Guignol punch or a James Bond blowout, a bankable commodity—and a cheap shot. Preposterous juxtapositions offer equally unexpected (if less overtly violent) results. Consider the hallucinatory spins on Fox TV's syndicated hit show "Ally McBeal," in which personal fantasies and loopy apparitions are played out parenthetically between scenes. Same-sex public toilets invite situational malaise on the one hand, comic intimacies on the other. It is an appropriate setting for the *sturm-und-drang* tendencies that typify programs like this one, populated by the kinds of over-educated, self-indulgent, upper-middle class professionals that viewers clearly yearn to watch. But when a fleeting, inappropriate thought is instantly visualized, the mind reels: miniature dancing babies, magnified wagging tongues, bodies shrinking and careening out of giant dumpsters—these are unexpected images that derive their power as much from displaced context as from dramatic content. The appeal is vicarious rather than violent. And the effect is indeed surreal.

SUGGESTIVE IMAGES: *Rethinking Beauty*

Capitalizing on the success of the Internet auction model, and proposing a woefully aberrant interpretation of Darwin's theory of natural selection, the controversial Website known as Ron's Angels (www.ronsangels.com) acknowledges both its debt to celebrity culture, and its love of beauty. ("We are excited by beauty," opines the editorial, which is flanked by photos of beautiful women in suggestive poses. "Why?") By offering up the healthy reproductive eggs of fashion models for auction, founder Ron Harris hopes to "reflect the determination to pass every advantage possible along to our descendants." Clickable images of models are prominently displayed on the site's homepage, where Harris offers his own personal view of the power of design in the interest of reproduction: "Now, modern science presents the miraculous possibility of improving ourselves," he writes,"... the highest bidder gets youth, beauty, and social skills." At the time of its launch last fall, this combination of Web evangelism and ethics-free scientific appropriation made enough heads (and stomachs) turn to warrant a barrage of media coverage: to date, over 5,000 articles and 200 television stations worldwide have featured this controversial site. Such sensationalism may not be so far from the Nike ads: it is still shocking, though the prevailing image is of a kind of exalted, and, in this case, highly commoditized beauty. And once again, it is nothing new: the novelty of electronic commerce notwithstanding, it is hardly the first time sexual imagery has been used to front a sales pitch. The result, incidentally, is both comic *and* disquieting.

It is December as I write this and my neighbor's trampoline has been retired from active duty. Her house is now festooned with Christmas decorations, clusters of miniature white lights illuminating the rooflines and lining the windowsills. It is like a cartoon house, all exaggerated geometries and magnified proportions. But as I drive by, the image I am left with is not about architecture. It is not about Christmas. The image in my mind is of two little girls dancing on a summer night with their beautiful young mother, their arms reaching up to embrace the sky as they leap, fearlessly, into the air.

Originally published in *The New Rebublic,* this essay traces the prolific career of Paul Rand, arguably the most celebrated American graphic designer of the twentieth century. The essay explores Rand's personal form of modernism and his role in creating a new visual language that revolutionized American design as both an art and a business. Includes a detailed analysis of the complex tensions framing Rand's identity as an artist, designer and businessman, and explores the enduring relevance of his work for American corporations, most notably for IBM.

: Paul Rand: The Modern Designer

Graphic design is the most ubiquitous of all the arts. It responds to needs at once personal and public, embraces concerns both economic and ergonomic, and is informed by numerous disciplines including art and architecture, philosophy and ethics, literature and language, politics and performance. Graphic design is everywhere, touching everything we do, everything we see, everything we buy: we see it on billboards and in Bibles, on taxi receipts and on Websites, on birth certificates and on gift certificates, on the folded circulars tucked inside jars of aspirin and on the thick pages of children's chubby board books. Graphic design is the boldly directional arrows on street signs and the blurred, frenetic typography on the title sequence to "E.R." It is the bright green logo for the New York Jets and the monochromatic front page of *The Wall Street Journal*. It is hang-tags in clothing stores, playbills in theatres, timetables in train stations, postage stamps and cereal box packaging, fascist propaganda posters, and junk mail. It is complex combinations of words and pictures, numbers and charts, photographs and illustrations that, in order to succeed, demand the clear thinking of a particularly thoughtful individual who can orchestrate these elements so that they all add up to something distinctive, or useful, or playful, or suprising, or subversive, or in some way truly memorable. Graphic design is a popular art, a practical art, an applied art and an ancient art. Simply put, it is the art of visualizing ideas.

Until the Second World War, graphic design was better known in the United States as commercial art. Performed by printers and typesetters, it was more vocation than profession, more a reflection of the economic realities of a newly industrialized culture than an opportunity to engage the creative expression of an individual or an idea. Unlike the experimentation that characterized design as it was being practiced and taught in Europe in the early years of this century—led by cubism and constructivism, pioneers of de Stijl and disciples of the Bauhaus—what we now think of as "graphic design" was, in this country, driven by the demands of commerce and fueled by the prospect of eliminating the economic hardships that had plagued the nation during the Depression. Commercial art was a service industry motivated by the same honorable objectives that characterized the average consumer: it sought to encourage stability, promote prosperity, and to maintain a generally happy, don't-rock-the-boat kind of aesthetic status-quo.

If these were indeed the values extolled by a collective, national consciousness, it is perhaps not surprising that a good deal of the design of printed matter dating from the years between the wars was dry, unimaginative, and predictable. This work was often cluttered and decorative: it is as if the use of ornament became a kind of aesthetic panacea, masking the greater cultural complexities marking this awkward, transitional age.

More perplexing still, such ornamentation was at direct odds with the streamlined simplicity that otherwise characterized so much of the artistic expression—including painting, music, and literature—being produced during this same fertile period. Then again, if we consider commercial art to be not a fine but a popular art, it fails equally as an adequate mirror of social history. With the great exception of pre-World War Two propaganda (which as a body of work suggests an altogether different aesthetic, evoking the dramatic urgency of a highly politicized and socially polarized nation) the typical outlets for what would eventually become graphic design produced, in the 1920s and 1930s, little in the way of truly noteworthy activity. It is, in a sense, a puzzling sort of hiccup on the timeline of design history: a period marked at once by great social change and negligible creative progress.

But by the early 1930s, a small but accomplished group of American and European expatriate designers began to experiment with new ways to approach the design of commercial printed matter. Combining the experimental formal vocabularies of their European peers with the material demands of American commerce, they helped inaugurate a new visual language that would revolutionize the role of design as both a service and an art. Of this group—which included Lester Beall, Bradbury Thompson, and Alexey Brodovich, among others—none was so accomplished, or would produce as many lasting contributions to this field as Paul Rand, arguably our most celebrated American graphic designer, who died in 1996 at the age of eighty-two.

More than any other designer of this century, Rand is credited with bringing the modernist design aesthetic to post-war America. Highly influenced by the European modernists—Klee and Picasso, Calder and Miró—Rand's formal vocabulary signalled the advent of a new era. Using photography and montage, cut paper, and what would later become known as "The New Typography"—asymmetrical typography that engaged the eye and activated the page—Rand rallied against the sentimentality of staid, commercial layouts and introduced a new, modified avant-garde style that spoke to the clever ideas and restrained minimalism that he had observed in such European design magazines as the German *Gebrauchsgraphik* and the English *Commercial Art*. To look at Rand's work today—work that dates from as much as half a century ago—is to observe how an idea can be distilled to its most salient form. The style is playful, the message immediate, the communication undeniably direct. The results are engaging, effective, and, memorable.

Born in 1914 in Brooklyn, the son of orthodox Jewish immigrants from Vienna, Rand began drawing as a child and went on to attend Pratt Institute, Parsons School of Design, and The New York Art Student's League, where he studied with George Grosz. He opened his own studio in 1935; two years later he was named Art Director of *Esquire*. Still in his twenties, he suffered a terrible loss when his identical twin brother, a jazz musician, died in an automobile accident; Rand's own divorce and subsequent remarriage followed not long after. During these personally turbulent years he remained busy designing layouts for *Apparel Arts* magazine, as well as covers for the anti-fascist magazine *Direction* where, between 1938 and 1941, he honed his editorial skills experimenting with increasingly complex political issues—the Nazi seizure of the Sudetenland, for example.

In 1941, at the age of twenty-seven, he left to join the William H. Weintraub advertising agency, where he would spend the next thirteen years producing ads for, among others, El Producto, Dubonnet, Orbach's, and Revlon. Rand was hired as the graphic design consultant for IBM in 1956 (the same year Josef Albers hired him to teach in the graduate design program at Yale) where he collaborated with Thomas Watson, Jr. and Eliot Noyes on the famous striped letterforms that are still in use today.

It is worth noting, too, that Rand was one of the few distinguished practitioners of graphic design who saw fit (or found time) to publish on the subject. A contributing essayist to numerous design publications here and abroad, Rand went on to publish four critically acclaimed books: *Thoughts on Design* (1946); *Paul Rand: A Designer's Art* (1985); *Design, Form and Chaos* (1994) and most recently, *From Lascaux to Brooklyn* (1996). Consequently, he was perhaps the only designer of his generation to stake out a truly theoretical position where graphic design is concerned. It is this more than anything else that distinguishes his writing and indeed, his lasting contributions to the study of graphic design.

If Paul Rand's work reflected the reductive formal vocabularies of modernist practice, it is also true that his thinking (and writing) mirrored the intellectual curiosity of modernist ideology. Preoccupied by certain recurring themes, his books typically consist of short, staccato-like essays in which he considers the fundamental factors that shape our understanding of visual communication. In each of his books, he scrutinizes the relationship between art and design, between design and aesthetics, and between aesthetics and experience. At length, he examines the role of intuition and ideas, the balance between form and function, and the universal language of geometry. These ideas (which he called the designer's *raison d'être*) were fundamental to his inquiry, if not equally fundamental to his lifelong search for creative, intellectual, and spiritual resolution as an artist, a designer, and a Jew.

Rand believed these philosophical and visual themes to be timeless: "My interest has always been in restating the validity of those ideas which, by and large, have guided artists since the time of Polyclitus," he writes. "It is the continuing relevance of these ideals that I mean to emphasize, especially to those who have grown up in a world of punk and graffiti." That these same ideas would resurface in each successive book is puzzling: one wonders whether the arguments were an open expression of Rand's passionate beliefs, or an attempt to validate them in the first place. Certainly, Rand was universally known for his blustering self-confidence—evident not only from his writing, but from the inflammatory public statements that made him so eminently quotable ("The development of new typefaces is a barometer of the stupidity of our profession"). It is, however, equally true that the fervent devotion with which he applied himself to the practice of design was itself influenced to a considerable degree by the events of his early life. Here, one can imagine how those events—disagreements with the family, the loss of a brother—were played out in the studio and on the typewriter, and how the promises of modernism—in which the harmony of formal relationships gesture to a higher order, and seek to embrace a purist ideal—might have held, for Rand, a kind of divine appeal.

And while it is true that Rand's celebration of pure form gestured to an economy of means that might well be characterized as quintessentially modern, it is also true that his resistance to new, more abstract forms of expression revealed itself repeatedly in his writings, in public lectures, and in interviews, thus branding him, in his final years, as outmoded and conservative. A lifelong advocate of the modernist axiom "less is more," Rand was often criticized, later in his career, for his rejection of contemporary design idioms: it is not surprising, perhaps, that for most of his professional life, the words most frequently associated with him were "irascible," "ornery" and "curmudgeon." Indeed—and true to form—the formal dedication in his last book reads: "To my friends and enemies."

It is likely, then, that Rand's resistance to changes in the design profession evidenced itself in a kind of renewed devotion to the principles he held most dear. To this end, the critic in him saw contemporary design practice as a postmodern free-for-all, in which sentiment and subjectivity supplanted logic and clarity of purpose. The teacher in him saw an opportunity to redefine and restate the great lessons of the modernist legacy: in this context, his writing has a tireless, autodiagnostic quality, in which he carefully articulates the fundamental components which enable ideas to be made visually manifest. And the artist in him saw the necessity of promoting the same exacting standards that he used not only to evaluate his own work, but to assess the quality of any great work of art. "The quality of the work always precedes everything else," he explained in an interview not long before his death, adding pointedly: "And the quality, of course, is my standard."

Throughout his books, Rand sustained his arguments through repetition and at times, dogmatic emphasis: consistent with the urgency of his modernist mentors, his literary style mirrored the passionate—if not utterly evangelical—rhetoric of the manifesto. Written primer-style on such topics as "The Beautiful and The Useful," "Design and the Play Instinct," and "Intuition and Ideas," Rand's essays were extensively illustrated by visual examples drawn from his own portfolio, and footnoted with citations from his equally extensive library. In this view, his arguments were able to gesture with perhaps greater intellectual scope as the ideas themselves were presented within more robust discussions: here, design was examined not as a disenfranchised art form, but as an inherently humanist discipline.

The idea that the value of design could be explained and enriched by accompanying notes on philosophy, art criticism, or political discourse thus became Rand's editorial bailiwick: to this end, his marginalia were rich with references to John Dewey, Bertrand Russell, Alfred North Whitehead, Henri Bergson, and Henry James. In more targeted appeals, Rand would reference the writings of Kant and Hegel or the teachings of Leger and Albers, or add other equally enlightening observations from an exotic sampling of social theorists, architectural critics and ex-Presidents (in his last book, he quotes Jimmy Carter). In spite of such breadth—or perhaps because of it—the core of his thinking was always rooted in graphic design.

"To design," Rand writes in *Design, Form and Chaos*, "is much more than simply to assemble, to order, or even to edit: it is to add value and meaning, to illuminate, to simplify, to clarify, to modify, to dignify, to dramatize, to persuade, and perhaps even to amuse. To design is to transform prose into poetry." For Rand, graphic design was poetry. It was rhythm, contrast, balance, proportion, repetition, harmony, and scale, a carefully orchestrated vocabulary of simple form, specific function, and symbolic content. In his vision, a circle could be a globe, an apple, a face, a stop sign; in his hands, a square became a gift-wrapped box (the UPS trademark), an Egyptian frieze (the IDEO trademark) or a child's toy (the Colorforms trademark). Over the course of a career that spanned more than six decades, Rand produced a prolific body of work that included advertising and posters, books and magazines, illustration and—perhaps most important—a host of memorable trademarks for such corporations as ABC, IBM, UPS, and Westinghouse. It is for these, more than anything, that he is best remembered, perhaps because, like the man who created them, they lasted for so long.

A trademark is a company's signature, an emblematic stamp of authenticity that establishes the company's name, and firmly communicates the qualities with which it seeks to identify itself publicly. It is circumscribed within the larger notion of positioning a company's personality through its material presence in a culture, and perhaps for this reason falls under the more comprehensive rubric of "Corporate Identity." The process of mediating the relationship between the pragmatic demands of the corporation and the formal requirements of its trademark is the principle task of the designer: for Rand, it was an ideal task, and one which showcased his greatest strengths. It demanded at once a serious attention to the value of intuition (visualizing the logo that must be recognized instantly by millions of people) and an equal attention to the importance of intellect (isolating the idea that must be distilled into its most salient, germane form.)

That said, the success of many (though not all) of these logos may be attributable to a handful of factors. First, Rand spent over a decade in advertising, where he developed an acute appreciation for the value of design in the interest of commerce. Working on short deadlines, collaborating with clients and copywriters (it is said that while working for the Weintraub Agency, he and William Bernbach personally pioneered the art-and-copy collaborative teams that are widely used in most agencies today), Rand quickly learned that design could function as a potent strategic tool. This experience did little to lessen his commitment to the importance of art and design: if anything, it reinforced his aesthetic and increasingly modernist leanings. But it also forced him to become ruthlessly pragmatic, even skeptical—qualities that made him particularly well-poised to understand the communications needs of corporations where he undertook the somewhat thorny task of determining what he called "the relevant idea and its formal interpretation." In the wake of his years spent reading, designing, and hacking his way through the advertising battlefields of post-war America, the challenges of corporate identity provided Rand with the ideal framework within which to test the validity of his combined talents and experience.

Second, Rand was blessed with good clients—and while he himself never claimed to be particularly good at business (he openly credited this skill to his wife, Marion), he made a point of approaching his projects with laser-beam focus. Given the tenor of the passionate ideas expressed in his writings, one can easily imagine Rand playing the aesthetic evangelist, and it is more than likely that he was instrumental in fostering his clients' vested interest in (and appreciation for) the importance of good design. "A company's reputation is very much affected by how it looks and how its products work," he writes in the essay "Good Design is Good Will." "A beautiful object that does not work is a reflection on the company's integrity. In the long run, it may not lose only its customers but its good will. Good design will no longer function as the harbinger of good business but as the herald of hypocrisy." Hypocrisy, it should be noted, was something Rand successfully avoided for the length of his career: consistent with his irascible demeanor, he was brutally honest with himself and everyone around him, including his clients. Steve Jobs reportedly once asked Rand to "design a few logos" for his then-start-up company, NEXT. "If you want a few logos then ask a few designers," Rand barked back. "But if you want me to solve your problem for you, I'll solve your problem for you." Such exchanges were typical of Rand's brusque negotiating style. Equally typical for Rand (but largely atypical for the industry in general) were the six-figure fees he was able to command for the design of single trademarks.

Third, Rand had the good fortune to work with clients who stayed in their jobs long enough to ensure the longevity of his creations. This may explain why the more enduring logos commissioned over thirty years ago—IBM (1956), Colorforms (1959), Westinghouse (1960), UPS (1961), and ABC (1962), for example—have remained virtually unchanged since their inception. Today, however, the peripatetic nature of corporate life makes such sustained activity considerably more difficult to achieve. The way business is conducted, too, has changed in keeping with new management strategies and new multidisciplinary teams; the way trademarks are used has changed in keeping with new products, activities, and services; and consequently, the very nature of corporate identity itself has evolved over the years as a response to such technological, social, commercial, and bureaucratic shifts. This discrepancy between Rand's formally isolationist view of the logo and these complex metamorphoses in business culture may explain in part why some of Rand's later logotypes—The Limited (1988) and Morningstar (1991), for instance—received less favorable public attention and achieved, consequently, less competitive success.

Certainly there have been (and are) other designers and design firms who have made enormous contributions to the practice of corporate identity. Pentagram, Landor Associates, and Chermayeff and Geismar are among several such firms here in the United States whose efforts have been widely recognized and whose role, in addition to the design of the mark itself, has grown to include market research, product positioning, and consumer branding. These firms typically work in teams and in collaboration with clients to determine the applications of an identity across a wide platform that may include, among other things, publications, collateral materials, signage, and packaging.

Rand, on the other hand, worked solo, and only with the chief person responsible for making the decisions. He was violently—and quite vocally—opposed to group dynamics of any kind, including focus groups and what he called "design by committee," either of which he believed added an unnecessary layer of complexity to an already diffcult process. In this way, he streamlined the workflow dynamic in much the same way that he distilled a design idea: it was a methodology that served him, and his clients, extremely well.

In the mid-50s, Rand produced his most successful logo, the trademark for IBM. Working closely with Eliot Noyes—then IBM's consulting director for design—Rand quickly understood that to be successful, what mattered was a flexible logo that could be interpreted as a system by different designers to suit different needs within the corporation. For Rand, this translated to a kind of modular thinking: taking his philosophical cues from architecture (and in particular, from the writings of Le Corbusier on similar principles in architecture) he experimented with proportion, scale, color, and humor. For the IBM logo, this translated to a basic equation in which the fundamental mark might be duplicated, rotated, colorized, or mutated in such a way as to play the variable against the constant. In 1970, he extended the boundaries of this notion to include an "eye-bee-m" pictogram that has been widely used in posters and promotional materials ever since. The trademark itself (commissioned by the conservative Thomas Watson, Jr., largely in response to its great competitor, Olivetti) was based on City Medium, an obscure typeface designed by George Trump in 1930. Rand designed the initial logo in 1956; four years later he added the stripes, in an effort to visually minimize the discrepancy in character widths between the narrow "i" and the wider "b" and "m." His inspiration in striping the letterforms came from observing the multi-lined striations on legal documents, used to discourage counterfeiting. By weighing up the stripes, Rand modernized the font, simplified the mark, and gestured to a kind of visual speed one might rightly associate with a technology company. (He also believed stripes had a universal appeal, evoking images including Romanesque architecture and Parisian fashion.) Rand went on to design both a thirteen-line and later an eight-line variation, which remains the basic corporate standard in use today.

IBM, however, is perhaps more the exception than the rule. Typically, Rand's programs were logo programs, not identity programs. They were trademark-based, not communication-based. His marks were simple, modern, geometric abstractions of letterforms, recognizable shapes and symbols. He designed them to work at any scale or at an angle, on the side of a truck or emblazoned on an annual report cover, but they were rarely conceived of as part of larger, more complex communications programs—designed to embrace evolution and permutation over time or across disparate media. To Rand, a modern mark was a simple mark, and the secret to making things last lay in keeping them simple. In keeping them simple, he was indeed able to lay claim to the greatest endurance record of any trademark designer to date: so while the Westinghouse logo was retooled five times between 1900 and 1953, Rand's 1960 redesign has remained intact for thirty-eight years. His 1961 logo for UPS has lasted almost as long.

Do these logos succeed where others fail merely because they are simple? Are they better because they are ubiquitous, making us recognize them faster and behave more efficiently as a result? Or do we tire of their inertia, demanding more from identity programs than predictability and sameness? Many classic marks that previously achieved success through widespread recognition—the bell in Bell

Telephone, for instance—have been given face-lifts in recent years. These upgraded marks may remain simple in theory, but in practice they reflect more complex uses and are, consequently, of a more idiosyncratic nature. It is interesting, too, to note the degree to which stripes, particularly in the mid-80s, started to take on a kind of visual identity of their own, gracing marks for such corporate giants such as AT&T (Saul Bass, 1984), Nynex (Lippincott and Margulies, 1984), and the traditionally depicted, though still striped, Prudential rock (Lee and Young, 1984).

Today's identity programs face even greater performance expectations as they compete for attention in a landscape dominated by increasingly kinetic media. Modernism notwithstanding, a timeless logo is, to some, little more than a tired logo. Consider UPS: fixed and predictable, a beige package trapped inside a heraldic shield on a flat, brown field. Once an emblem of solid reliability, today it is to some little more than a gloomy graphic portrait of snail mail—a fact somewhat exacerbated by the clean look and no-nonsense efficiency of its greatest competitor, Federal Express, reborn not long ago as "FedEx" in a cheery orange-and-purple identity program redesigned by Landor Associates. Or think ABC: compared to NBC's fluttering peacock, or CBS's blinking eye, Rand's 1962 logo is surprisingly static fare for television—a modernist bubble sporting Bauhaus typography, but static nonetheless.

Clearly, to design a modern mark forty years ago was a very different task. The corporate America into which Rand was introduced in the 1950s and 60s was eager to define itself within the context of a relatively new—and rapidly growing—consumer culture. Rand's penchant for purism gave visual form to the exalted ideals of corporate leaders whose great ambition was to embrace new and complex audiences: this process involved rethinking traditional methods of corporate communication which, in the years directly following the Second World War, had been largely characterized by unimaginative marketing efforts and unnecessarily decorative design. Given a climate ripe for change, the idea that visual communication could be both powerful and simple was a radical—but fashionably pragmatic—idea.

But more important even than this was Rand's unusual capacity to express an idea verbally. For his corporate clients, he habitually prepared detailed reports in which he presented a new trademark as a carefully documented process, illustrating the evolution of his ideas over time and articulating his argument with clarity and purpose. In these eloquently written reports, what was perhaps most striking was his decision to expose the design process. The writing is a lyrical mix of intention, comparison, description, and analogy: here, Rand celebrated the integration of reasoning with the presentation of graphic design. Rather than minimizing the impact of his conclusions, such thoughtful discourse reinforced his visual thinking by positioning his ideas within a broader cultural context. By removing his argument from the immediate corporate climate it was intended primarily to address, and by distancing it from the broader demographic audience it was intended ultimately to reach, he gestured to a larger, more universal world. In the process, Rand used a clear formal vocabulary in precisely the way his mentors would have intended, as an international language: cross-cultural, timeless, and accessible to all. Rand called these reports the "musical accompaniment" to design.

Looking back on his prolific career, it is paradoxical to think that the man who gave graphic life to such technological giants as IBM (with whom he retained the esteemed position of graphic design consultant for over thirty-five years), IDEO (the international technology think-tank based in Northern Caifornia), and Steve Jobs' NEXT should himself have been so averse to the computer. How could Rand, the devout modernist, be so openly resistant to the progressive changes brought about by the machine—the symbolic child of modern industry? It is as though the same geometric forms that embodied the logic of mechanical reproduction, the same formal vocabulary that inspired his mentors and defined the very spirit of modernism was available to Rand only in theory.

Such contradictions underscored his entire career, if not his entire life, and they are everywhere present in his writing. Quoting William J. R. Curtis on Le Corbusier in "Good Design is Good Will," Rand writes: "It is necessary to understand history, and he who understands history knows how to find continuity between that which was, that which is, and that which will be." A moment later he discourages any reference to historical precursorism, and quotes the British philosopher Karl Popper: "The past is only an indication," he writes, "not an explanation." And what of the contradictions in his own personal history? The darling of corporate America for decades, Rand rejected the lure of city life, opting to work alone, in his Connecticut home studio for the better part of his career; while he openly claimed to despise academia, he remained a devoted member of the Yale faculty for more than a quarter century; and despite the painful consequences of his family's extreme religious standards, he remained an observant Jew for the whole of his life. It is likely that the orthodoxy that characterized both his relationship to design and his relationship to God was an attempt to equalize these polarities, to right the balances, to establish order in the studio as well as in the spirit.

Yet here too there were contradictory impulses: "Five is better than four, three is better than two," Rand often announced to his students, claiming that the mind worked harder and received a greater sense of reward when optically resolving asymmetrical relationships on the page. As he grew older, such lessons were taught with even greater passion and emphasis. At the same time, in his own work, the pioneering spirit which led him to push the boundaries of expression on magazine covers and in advertisements in the 1930s and 1940s—the poetic interpretations, the playful juxtapositions—grew decidedly less ambitious. And with each successive book, the editorial organization is looser, the type is larger, and the writing is weaker. Rand's last book, *From Lascaux to Brooklyn,* is in many ways the weakest book of all, and has certainly been the least favorably received. Here, the precision that qualified the earlier essays is missing, the ideas follow a less logical path, and the bibliographic marginalia are an eclectic mix of philosophy, aesthetics, and literature combined somewhat randomly with Rand's brazen, ex-cathedra statements. At the same time, it is in many ways his greatest work: passionate, exuberant, without question a remarkable achievement for anyone at the age of eighty-one. "The impulse to creation knows no exception—fashionable or practical," he writes. "Cosmetics or jewelry, flatware or footwear, hammers or nails—it is the urge to solve problems, visual or mechanical, that really matters." It is also a fitting final achievement for such an accomplished life: this is Rand going out in a blaze of glory.

If the combination of intellectual curiosity and street-smart skepticism caused Rand to question everything in general, teaching provided him with the ideal opportunity to do so within the very specific context of a first-rate academic institution. Paul Rand taught at Yale for more than thirty-five years, and this essay examines the evolution of his very peculiar (and successful) pedagogical approach: from pragmatic assignments in the early 1960s that invited students to redesign boxes of laundry soap and packages of chewing gum to more abstract compositional exercises involving typography, geometry, and pared-down color palettes, Rand's seminal influence on American design education reflects the fascinating permutations of his own distinguished career.

: Paul Rand: The Modern Professor

There is a story about Paul Rand as a young man (which is unlikely to be apocryphal since he used to tell it about himself), in which he recalled having had the opportunity to spend time with his great mentor, Le Corbusier, on a European beach one sunny afternoon. The eager young Rand plied the older master with questions about form and system and design principles, prompting an impulsively honest—if exasperated reply. "Young man," said Le Corbusier, jumping into the ocean, "you are simply too serious!"

In spite of the playfulness for which his work is so often remembered, Rand was indeed extremely serious about many things: about art and design and geometry, about history and ethics, about psychology, perception, and form-giving. He never tired of certain fundamental questions, and never stopped questioning himself and those around him about the appropriateness, the applicability, and the purpose of design. He hated trickery, decoration and trends, superfluous touches and cosmetic effect. He strove for purity, efficiency and durability, clarity and purpose, simplicity and practicality. Paul Rand—intellectually restless, creatively insatiable—was a wonderful teacher because he never stopped being a student. This also explains why he was loved by so many and feared by so many, and why he was so utterly impossible to please.

He was, like many fascinating and fiercely intelligent people, a man of enormous complexity and great contradiction. Perhaps the greatest gaps lay in the spaces between his writing and his teaching: both lifelong passions that would seem, almost by necessity, to have been interconnected, and yet they were not. As a writer, Rand expressed his insights with an eloquence that was rarely (if ever) matched in the classroom: here he was impatient, easily distracted, and often resistant to discourse. His writing, too, was peppered with references to a broad and interdisciplinary bibliography; yet this bibliography, though offered as a handout to those students who doggedly pursued him, was never truly integrated into the scope of his curricula. (It is worth noting, too, that Rand's bibliography changed and grew considerably over the years: while the 1965 version included a comprehensive section on gestalt psychology, later versions included more abundant literary references, more architectural sources, and many more periodicals.) Rand favored certain key texts which he recycled again and again in his assignments: many former Yale students, for example, remember a classic publication-design problem based on the seminal 1920 Le Corbusier/Ozenfant essay "On the Plastic in Art."

Perhaps most puzzling of all, Rand's exhaustive knowledge of art history, which was perpetually well-documented in his books, seldom found its way into his classroom: here, he never showed slides, never lectured, never made conscious, explicit reference to the sources that lay at the very core of his own intellectual pursuits, his own self-made education. "When I saw his library later in his life and all the other things that he studied and looked at I was stunned," recalls Virginia Smith (Yale MFA '58), now Chair of Design at Baruch College in New York. "There was never a clue about that in class." Former Netscape Design Director Hugh Dubberly (Yale MFA '83) concurs: "It surprised me that such an articulate writer could be so tongue-tied in person."

Perhaps, in the end, Rand felt that it was up to the students to resolve these gaps, to find their own sources of inspiration, much as he had done—and indeed, continued to do. While never articulated as such, it is likely that he presupposed in his students a certain degree of capability, independence, and resourcefulness that would likely lead them to their own conclusions. His role was to guide them, to instill in them certain basic principles, and to encourage them to become demanding and objective editors of their own work. In this he was ruthless—and indeed, unparalleled. That he remains for so many students their most memorable professor is, consequently, not at all surprising.

Rand's own education was uneven: He was essentially self-taught. "When I went to school my education was lackadaisical. There was no system," he once said. "When I studied with George Grosz (at the New York Art Student's League) in the 1930s, he had just come over from Europe, and he didn't speak a word of English. You can imagine what his classes were like. He walked around and looked at your work and made a few marks, and you wondered what he was driving at. I'm still wondering." Rand would later go on to attend Pratt Institute, The Parsons School of Design, and The Art Student's League in New York. He taught briefly and sporadically at Pratt, Cooper Union, and The New York Lab School before being invited to Yale as a visiting critic in 1956; soon afterward he was offered a formal appointment in The School of Art, a position he would retain until his retirement in 1993.

Looking back, given the breadth of his interests and the serious-ness with which he pursued them, it seems somehow inevitable that Rand would come to a place like Yale to teach. At that time—the mid-1950s—the schools of Art and Architecture included a number of European refugees and Bauhaus disciples, among them Josef Albers, who had been recruited by Louis Kahn to come to Yale several years earlier to head its art department. Albers had long advocated the benefits of interdisciplinary study in the arts, and from the beginning, graphic design students were required to study photography and printmaking, typography, print production, drawing and painting, as well as the famous Albers color course—affectionately referred to by the students as "spots and dots." Soon after his own arrival at Yale, Albers appointed Alvin Eisenman to direct the department of Graphic Design, and together they extended the faculty to include a number of distinguished visiting critics, including, among others, Lester Beall, Leo Lionni, Alexey Brodovich, Walker Evans, Bradbury Thompson, Herbert Matter, and Rand, who came on the recommendation (and following the departure) of Alvin Lustig. (The practice of engaging a rotating stable of outside critics continues in the MFA program at Yale to this day.)

If the combination of intellectual curiosity and street-smart skep-ticism caused Rand to question everything in general, teaching provided him with the ideal opportunity to do so within the very specific context of a first-rate academic institution. Here, differences of opinion with his esteemed colleagues were rarely concealed; if anything, such conflicts helped to cement his growing convictions about the most effective ways to teach graphic design. Principal among these conflicts, in the early days, were his disagreements with Paul Rudolph, then Dean of Architecture at Yale.

To begin with, Rudolph was opposed to grades. Recalls Eisenman, "Rudolph thought the idea of grading a work of art was too vulgar for words." Rand, on the other hand, completely objected to the idea of abandoning grades. His own challenging experience as a student at Pratt had led him to believe that there was enormous value in rewarding the deserving—and, by conjecture, in punishing those who did poorly. Another bone of contention lay in the studio model itself. Rudolph favored the notion of the open studio (meaning that students could come and go somewhat freely during the class critique), a policy Rand objected to quite strongly, feeling that he could not possibly talk to students in an atmosphere where they were free to come and go as they pleased. (He later confessed to Eisenman that one of the reasons he felt this way was that the Rabbi would never have stood for it!)

From the beginning, the Rand studios at Yale were framed within a certain prescribed set of rules. If at first these rules were functional—students were graded and were required to stay put—they later grew to include more formal and procedural limitations. Later, it was not uncommon for Rand to ordain which fonts could (and could not) be used, which techniques were objectionable, which presentation materials were acceptable, and so forth. In an effort to universalize and further objectify these notions, Rand looked for confirmation outside the narrow confines of the profession: here is where the doctrines of modernism offered structure, discipline, and a certain fundamental reasoning which Rand believed to be enormously applicable to the practice of graphic design.

This discipline—let's call it the study of limited means—would remain central to Rand's teaching for the next thirty-five years. The fact that he would continue to refine the rigors of such thinking reflected not only his dedication to teaching, but also the seriousness with which he approached art in general—and design in particular. Yet ironically, while there is a clear trajectory in the evolution of his own professional career, Rand's teaching methodology would undergo significant changes between the mid-50s and the mid-80s. Most interesting, the reasons and explanations for these changes (and there are several) reveal more about Rand as a modernist than perhaps anything else.

There were personal influences—from colleagues and mentors, among them Josef Albers, Le Corbusier, and Josef Müller-Brockmann. There were professional influences—particularly in the corporate arena, as Rand would begin to develop formal vocabularies and design

systems for such clients as Westinghouse and IBM. There were ideological influences—derived from his own reading and from observing the
teaching methodologies of other members of the Yale faculty,
including Alvin Eisenman, Armin Hoffman, and Herbert Matter. And,
there were certain to have been practical influences, in which Rand
would begin to adapt his problems to yield more satisfying and,
indeed, successful results among his students. Ultimately, to trace the
evolution of his teaching style over the course of more than thirty years
illuminates the strength of Rand's ability to identify the most germane
principles underlying the study of graphic design. This was undoubt-
edly his greatest strength as an educator, and remains, for many
former students, his most memorable and lasting gift.

In the beginning, Rand's assignments were typically product-
specific, tending to mirror projects he might have been engaged in in
his own studio: the design of an El Producto cigar box (1958), for
example, or a re-design of a can label for DelMonte pineapple (1960).
Chris Pullman, (Yale MFA '66), Vice President for Design at WGBH-TV
Boston, recalls being asked to design the packaging for Duz soap
flakes, and the real-world market analysis that followed. "We made
boxes and took them to the store," he remembers, "then we put them
up on shelves and examined them." Other Rand assignments during
this period included children's books (nursery rhyme collections and
vocabulary primers); calendars and posters; trademarks and
stationary; record jackets; book jackets; as well as packaging for choco-
late (Whitman's), coffee (Maxwell House) and wine (Château LaFitte
Rothschild). While attention was always paid to solutions that would
communicate with clarity, these early assignments were articulated
with perhaps less of an emphasis on formal issues *per se:* indeed,
many of them read like briefs from a client or specifications for a
printer, the problems stated with no-nonsense brevity, presented
with staccato-like parameters outlining size, shape, and printing limitations. "Redesign the package for Spearmint-flavored diet sugarless
gum using the existing size, copy, materials, and printing process,"
reads one of Rand's more prosaic project statements from this era. "A
memorandum from the manufacturer is posted in the drafting room."

Over time, however, Rand began to back away from these more
commercial projects, leaning instead toward a more principle-

oriented, rational, and increasingly formal approach to teaching design. This transition—some have even referred to it as a sea-change—occurred sometime in the early 1960s, and marked what Chris Pullman has called "Rand's transformation from a nuts-and-bolts guy to a true theorist."

By the mid-60s, Rand began to pay specific attention to the way a problem itself was given. Some ten years after he first began teaching at Yale, he expressed these views in the now-celebrated essay, "Design and the Play Instinct." "I believe that if, in the statement of a problem, undue emphasis is placed on freedom and self-expression, the result is apt to be an indifferent student with a meaningless solution," he writes. "Conversely, a problem with defined limits, implied or stated disciplines which are, in turn, conducive to the instinct of play, will most likely yield an interested student and, very often, a meaningful and novel solution."

Rand thus came to believe that the success of a given problem lay largely in the way it was articulated—and the limitations within which it was given. In "Arts and the University," a video documentary produced by WGBH-TV Boston in 1964, Rand explained it this way: "There are restrictions which are built in both by the student, by the client, and by the teacher, which tend to help the student solve the problem." He would later amend this thinking even further: "If possible," he wrote in a subsequent problem statement, "teaching should alternate between theoretical and practical problems—between those with tightly stated 'rules' imposed by the teacher and those with rules implied by the problem itself."

Many of the projects Rand assigned during the 1960s reflect this yearning for—and struggle with—a practical/theoretical balance. A good, though unusual, example (it was only given twice) is an assignment he gave to redesign the classic game of Parcheesi. Here, students were asked to abide by the strict rules of the game—a discipline that presaged the sorts of guidelines Rand would later impose upon other assignments, made more interesting, perhaps, by the fact that the game itself carried with it its own implicit and extremely particular set of rules. The Parcheesi project is significant for several reasons, not least of which lies in its dual appeal to qualities Rand would return to—in his own work as well as in his teaching—again and again:

simplicity and playfulness. In retrospect, it was an early and comparatively radical exercise both in information design and interaction
design (students were required to design both the game and its rule
book). The results were playful, unusual, and, in some cases, extraordi-
narily beautiful.

As Rand's emphasis shifted away from a product orientation, and
toward exposing the underlying principles that collectively defined
the practice of graphic design, the gap between teaching and writing
began to grow narrower. While his bedside manner remained virtually unchanged, Rand's project statements came to be articulated with
more exuberance, more specificity, and a great deal more thought.
They grew longer, more detailed, more cross-discliplinary—and at the
same time, more didactic. It was not uncommon for the text to be
punctuated by declarations of the master's own non-negotiable
design values: "Literal interpretations should be avoided," "Initiation is
more effective than imitation," and the classic, incontestable
"Originality is more a question of how than what" were among some
of the authoritative statements Rand's students grew to know inti-
mately. Most important for the professor, these assignments (given
over and over again) gave him the opportunity to fine-tune his ideas,
his rationales, and his principles. Consequently, the assignments
themselves became much more focused. For the students, they
became not only more clear, but more valuable and indeed, more
widely applicable. "Mr. Rand's class assignments were a marvel,"
recalls Hugh Dubberly. "His presentation of the problems was brief
and clear. He constrained the assignments so well that it was difficult
to do poor work."

Rand's later assignments were, in a sense, intellectual explorations
of the study of limited means—a pedagogical celebration of the
modernist ideal. Twenty years after his diet gum assignment, Rand
delivered the following project statement: "The object of this problem
is to sharpen your awareness of form and its relation to color and
content," it began. "It is the abstract, non-representational, two-dimensional quality of letters paired with content, that make the use of words
so meaningful in modern painting and graphic design. The poetry of
Mallarmé, the collages of Picasso, and the typographic antics of the
futurists have revealed the poetic side of familiar words." Such

language introduced a series of assignments that would soon become known as the Visual Semantics Projects.

"The term visual semantics refers to the meaning and manipulation of words (letters) to illustrate an idea, action or the evocation of an image," Rand writes in his preface to the problem statement. "The word serves a dual purpose, verbal and pictorial. This involves the arrangement of letters in such a way as to make a word visually self-explanatory—a kind of universal sign language." In perfecting the assignment, Rand experimented with word choices: in the early years, for example, students worked with the words "Mask," "Banjo," and "Circus." It is likely that, over time, Rand became more intrigued with the notion of asking students to explore the visual dynamics of the letterforms particularly, with regard to the work of certain artists: for example, "Banjo" and Picasso, or "Circus" and Calder. (Rand later moved away from word-ideas and toward proper names themselves, later assigning "Miró" and finally settling on "Leger.")

Students thus created visual compositions that reflected the supporting principles of a given artist's style rather than mimicking the artist's work itself. For Rand, this project effectively illustrated the value of principle-based teaching in a manner that was at once simple (students worked only with cut paper and glue) and succinct (students distilled their complex ideas into pure typography). "It always had to do with the letters," recalls Philip Burton, now Associate Professor of Graphic Design at University of Illinois at Chicago, who taught at both Yale and in Brissago with Rand and Armin Hoffman during these years. "It always had to do with seeking to capture the essence of the artist—whatever the student perceived that to be."

The visual semantics exercises would become, in effect, Rand's signature projects, and formed the basis for the curriculum he would later develop, with Hoffman, at Yale's summer program in Brissago, Switzerland, which began in 1977 and continued until the early 1990s. Here, Rand typically spent an intensive week in a studio with approximately fifteen students and, unlike the Yale studios, no technology—no stat camera, no computers, nothing. Recalls Nancy Mayer (Yale MFA '84) now principal of Mayer+Myers, Philadelphia: "It was a big deal that there was nothing but pencil and paper. Plus, we had a week with Rand all day every day: this in itself was a shockingly different experience.

What Brissago offered was total immersion in a project. The total immersion over that period of time is a very different educational experience." The intensity of the Brissago environment offered Rand a kind of concentrated laboratory within which to teach: Here, he was in an ideal position to focus his students' attention on precisely the kinds of formal values he believed lay at the core of a serious—and lasting—design education. "Paul was thrilled with the work that the students accomplished there," recalls Burton. "He was thrilled with every single aspect of it. He would tell me, 'this is the way graphic design should be taught.'"

It is important to note that Rand was not alone in this thinking: Indeed, many of his colleagues at Yale shared this concern for narrowing the focus, isolating the ideas and crafting assignments that would elicit a sharper understanding of the underlying principles of design—whereas the more product-specific problems seemed to allow students to bypass these principles. "One of the things I found was that it was getting sort of boring to give yet another book jacket assignment," recalls Alvin Eisenman. "It didn't result easily in learning about the principles—and the only thing that made a real difference was learning about the principles. Rand wasn't alone in this, of course. Rand and Brad Thompson and Herbert Matter and myself—we all believed in the importance of design principles."

Looking beyond the parameters of the design department, the considerable influence that Josef Albers lent to students and faculty alike may also have been a significant factor in Rand's decision to move toward a more principle-based teaching strategy. As Rob Roy Kelly (Yale MFA '55), former Chair of Graphic Design at Arizona State University in Tempe, writes in "The Early Years of Graphic Design at Yale University," Albers had "the ability to teach formal values in a manner which stimulated students to becomes more visually aware."

Perhaps the member of the Yale design faculty who was most focused on the translation of formal values in the context of graphic design education was Armin Hoffman. His own classes centered on concentrated exercises in which students practiced hand skills (working with brushes, mixing color, and drawing type) the intended result of which was to fine-tune their ability to see. It is likely that Rand's move away from practical and towards more formal coursework was significantly influenced by Hoffman, whose curricula at the Kunstgewerbeschule in Basel were based on similar principles of rational, systems-oriented thinking. But true to form, it is likely that Rand disagreed with Hoffman as much as (if not more than) he agreed with him.

To begin with, there were disagreements about the way class problems were framed, and the amount of time within which they were expected to be completed—if they were to be completed at all. "Rand very much believed that a project must have a very definite resolution within a specific time frame," recalls Chris Myers (Yale MFA '83) now principal, Mayer+Myers, and Chair of Graphic Design at University of the Arts in Philadelphia. "He referred to Armin's approach as 'the endless problem'—in other words, that every solution generated more solutions. For Rand, understanding and coming to a conclusion was itself an enormously valuable lesson. And Rand believed that you had to make a decision." Indeed, Rand felt that students should be given projects with a clear path of problem-solving—problems with a beginning, a middle, and an end. Quoting Alfred North Whitehead on this topic, Rand once wrote: "The pupils have got to be made to feel they are studying something, and not merely executing intellectual minuets."

Rand was also a much tougher critic than Hoffman. This is well substantiated among more than thirty years of former students, many of whom share vivid memories of running from the studio in tears after a particularly grueling Rand critique. ("I don't know of any other way of teaching Art except by criticizing," Rand once remarked.) Eisenman recalls requesting a more compassionate review process, telling Rand that if he continued in this manner the school would be required to "put in drains in the studio floor for all the tears." This harshness was especially apparent in Brissago: unlike at Yale, where he habitually met with only two or three students at a time, Rand met with the entire studio in one room, passing from desk to desk to critique students individually. "He was blunt," recalls Myers, "and he would say something in an even tone but it would send a lot of people running from the room in tears. You'd hear him from the other side of the room, evaluate your own work in the context of what he was saying and then, all at once, you would start hearing the sound of sixteen people trying to crumple their sketches quietly and start over."

Rand's growing interest in grid systems was also the source of some debate and consequent influence during these years. Derived from conversations with Hoffman, from his reading of the seminal studies published by Josef Müller-Brockmann in the late 1960s, and from his work with Ken Hiebert and others at Westinghouse during this same period, Rand was immediately taken in by the formal appeal to structure and system, the modularity, the harmony, and the balance which came from understanding the design, development, and proper application of the typographic grid. "Rand's systems interests had been stimulated early on by Le Corbusier's *Le Modulor* and the Japanese Tatami Mat system," recalls Ken Hiebert, founding Chair of Graphic Design at University of the Arts, "but 1965 seemed to be a time of zeroing in on typographic grid systems in his own work and teaching."

In the classroom in particular, the applications of the grid were of enormous consequence. "The publications project was really about learning the value of a grid system," notes Myers, adding that Rand's particular interest was in "the idea of how much structure is necessary to carry an idea and to carry form." Interestingly, Rand continued to be fueled by his disagreements with others: for example, although he advised his students to read the book and judge for themselves, he openly opposed the fundamental orthodoxy with which Müller-Brockmann approached this material. For many students, this controversy between a structural principle and its formal application made the grid problems especially challenging. Yet ironically, in spite of his capacity for intellectual analysis, Rand's equally fervent need to simplify everything caused him to resist some of the more complex verbal and mathematical reasoning which the Europeans systematically brought to their grid evocations. Recalls Hiebert, "Rand was easily overwhelmed by brilliant Swiss and German grid manifestations, but his own language didn't fit the technical substrate. He kept it in very simple, humane, often childlike terms. There was something about Rand that resisted the technical as much as he admired it. In no case did he want to get bogged down with the technical."

While it is easy to assume Rand's technical resistance was generational, it turns out to have had more to do with his modernist tendencies than perhaps anything else. Ever the purist, he believed all processes—mechanical, technical, or otherwise—should be as neutral as possible: consequently, he viewed the celebration of modern technology, particularly in the studio and among his students, as enormously suspect. "The quality issuing from any process, mechanical or otherwise, is a reflection of that particular process, and the visual effect (style) is closely related to it," he once wrote. "The more neutral the technique, the simpler the solution—unencumbered by eccentricities or confusing (he later changed this to "sentimental") associations."

Finally, given the zeal with which Rand had long followed the pursuits of the European modernists, and given the breadth of his own sizeable (and constantly expanding) library, it is indeed possible that Rand's decision to move toward more formal instruction in the studio was considerably influenced by his own reading. As with everything else, he continued to question his findings, to filter them through his own understanding of what made for good design. In the end, the designer always won: "Paul's eye was constantly prioritized for the aesthetic," Hiebert remembers, "and he allowed no distractions." To this end, Rand willingly adopted certain tenets of formalism—even the "gridism" espoused by his Swiss colleagues—but only insofar as they serviced the emerging principles underlying his own design philosophies. Of course, these philosophies radiated to an audience much wider than the privileged minority who attended Yale and Brissago, due in no small part to Rand's significant accomplishments as a writer. As in his teaching, Rand wrote to zero in on what was important, to make sense of the complexity of the world—not to oversimplify, but to assess, to understand and finally, to interpret. The strength of his focused observations lay at the core of much of this writing, and the lessons therein remain surprisingly applicable, despite the degree to which design (much like life itself) has, in recent years, had to adapt to an increasingly complex and technologically sophisticated consumer society.

Yet here too, the clarity of his thinking continues to impress and astonish us. "As I flipped through Rand's books I was humbled by the power with which he manipulated space and at the same time struck by the clarity of his accompanying prose," recalls John Maeda, Professor of Aesthetics and Computation at the MIT Media Lab. "I was immediately inspired to pursue the field of Graphic Design, not necessarily pertaining to the computer." At Maeda's request, Rand was invited to lecture at the Media Lab exactly forty years after he was first invited to Yale; and in a pattern that virtually duplicated his early days at Yale, a formal teaching appointment followed. In a triumphant, if poignant conclusion to his life as an educator, Rand willingly accepted this position, but due to his failing health, was unable to fulfill his promise. He died less than two weeks later.

In the end, of course, Rand's strength of conviction about design principles was incontestable. It was apparent in his teaching and his writing, to his colleagues and his clients, to those who read and will continue to read his books for generations to come. "That attitude was just hardwired in him," recalls Chris Pullman. "That complete conviction about issues formal and relational is, I think, one of the things that makes a memorable and great person. You know where a person stands. And Rand definitely stood for something."

Essay commissioned for the second edition of David Carson's
The End of Print, and written to my then-two year-old daughter,
in the style of Fay Weldon's "Letters to Alice on First Reading Jane
Austen." In discussing the finer points of interpretive typography,
the essay references Gertrude Stein, *Goodnight Moon*, particle
physics, and refrigerator magnets.

: Sticks and Stones Can Break My Bones but Print Can Never Hurt Me: A Letter to Fiona on First Reading
The End of Print WITH APOLOGIES TO FAY WELDON, JANE AUSTEN, AND DAVID CARSON

21 March 2000

Dear Fiona:

You are turning two in a few weeks and I think it's high time you understood a thing or two about graphic design. After all, you are part of Generation ABC and what are **ABC**s, after all, but typography?

And what is typography, you ask?

A good question.

Typography is letters (and numbers) and why they look the way they do. Sometimes letters are **BIG AND LOUD** and sometimes letters are small and quiet. Typography can make words look good. It can also make words look bad. But the way they look—whether they're pink or purple or big or small or quiet or noisy or happy or scary or funny or weird, well, that's something that comes from typography.

Which is also called *type*.

Which is sometimes called *print*.

Which is a word that occasionally causes people to wrinkle up their noses and describe a time when it was customary to wear burlap shoes and sit hunched over, by candlelight, scratching painstakingly written messages to one's friends and neighbors using quill pens. This really happened, back in ancient times. Like back when there were mummies and dinosaurs. Before television. Like when Daddy was little.

Printing is what you do when you write letters one at a time, as opposed to script, which is when you write letters so-that-they-connect-to-each-other-like-this. Printing is also used to describe what happens when machines (called presses) get hold of all those words, all that typography, and actually press the letters, together, onto paper.

Paper is a word that occasionally causes people to wrinkle up their noses and describe a time when it was customary to wear burlap shoes and sit hunched over, by candlelight, scratching painstakingly written messages to one's friends and neighbors using quill pens. This really happened, back in ancient times. Like back when there were word processors and 8-track tapes. Before computers. Like when Mommy was little.

Now here's the really confusing part. A lot of people say print is dead. Flat and not moving. Dead, like when we drive down our road and see a rabbit or a woodchuck that didn't make it across in time? The whole concept of roadkill is something I had hoped to put off for a few years, but I think it's important for us to get clear about one thing.

Print isn't dead, sweetheart. It's just sleeping.

So as you begin to learn your **ABC**s, remember that your mind is like a giant alarm clock that wakes those letters up so that they spell something, so that they mean something, whether they're on TV or in a book or scratched on the side of a wall somewhere. And while you're at it, remember that **S** isn't the same as **5** and **I** isn't the same as **1**. Remember that **1 L0V3 U** isn't the same as **I LOVE YOU** even though it looks cool. Remember that anything that looks cool probably won't look cool for very long. Remember that very long means, well, probably about a day-and-a-half. Remember that pictures may speak louder than words, but that words speak volumes. Remember that sometimes typography can help you understand something or react to something or feel a certain way faster, but that it probably won't help resolve conflicts between embittered nations or advance your capacity for reason or prevent you from getting bee stings or tick bites or chicken pox. Remember that spelling mistakes are celebrated in email but not tolerated in literature. Remember that literature is made up of stories that are what they are because someone wrote them down, letter by letter, word by word, intending for them to be read and remembered and retold for years and years and years to come. Remember that this is why your father and I want you to learn your **ABC**s, in the order in which they were intended to be learned, even though you can, and will, mix up the magnets on the refrigerator to proudly spell words like **HRLDGSNO** and **WSIGEFOO** and **PSTWE12O2GE**. Someday when you read the work of Gertrude Stein or look at the work of David Carson you will make sense of such verbal and visual and perceptual aberrations, but until then, my sweet girl, remember that your **ABC**s are what helps you to read, and reading is what opens up your mind so that you can learn about anything you want. Turtles. Communism. Particle physics. Reading feeds your brain and helps your mind to grow. So today's *Goodnight Moon* is tomorrow's *Charlotte's Web* is next year's *Elmer and the Dragon* and before you know it you'll be reading Thomas Hardy and Thomas Mann and A. S. Byatt and V. S. Naipaul, just as your parents did, and our parents did and with any luck, your children will. And even though we read them printed on paper and you will very likely read them emblazoned on a screen, do you know what, Fiona? It doesn't matter, because no matter what the typography does (or doesn't do), and no matter what print is (or isn't), words are just ideas waiting to be read. And reading will never die. Reading is your ticket to the world.

Index

: Glossary

ACTION ITEMS: things on an agenda or priority list that need action **AFFINITY GROUPS:** self-sufficient support systems of people with common interest **ATM:** automated teller machine **BANDWIDTH:** the amount of data that can be passed along a communications channel in a given period of time **BANNER ADS:** images containing advertising content that can be clicked on **BRANDING:** a device that telegraphically communicates product benefits to consumers to achieve perceptions that will deliver sustainable competitive advantage **CD-ROM:** compact disk–read only memory **CSF:** critical success factor **CLICK-THROUGHS:** the number of people that click on a banner ad; a percentage of total number of banner ads clicked on divided by total number of banner ads displayed **DATA MINING:** database applications that look for hidden patterns to determine previously unknown relationships within groups of data **DRILL-DOWNS:** technique of navigating through a tree structure in a directory from broad categories to specific categories **EYEBALLS:** people **HDTV:** high definition television **HRS:** human resources strategies **HTML:** hypertext mark-up language describing the content of a page in terms of display and degree of interaction **HYPERTEXT:** special type of database system in which objects such as text, pictures, or music can be creatively linked to each other **IMAX:** image maximum, a motion picture format **KPI:** key performance indicator **LMS:** lifestyle management services **MARK-UP LANGUAGE:** a collection of elements used to indicate the structure and format of a document; a language that contains mark-up symbols to describe the contents of a page or file **MINDSHARE:** the process of penetrating the consumer's mind with a particular company or product **PDA:** personal digital assistant; electronic handheld information device **RAM:** random access memory **SGML:** standard generalized mark-up language **TIVO:** "TV your way" **TV:** apparatus that receives electromagnetic waves and displays reconverted images on a screen **TVML:** programming language that describes interactive TV programming display **UBV:** unique brand value **USER:** person **URL:** uniform resource locator; world wide web address **VCR:** videocassette recorder **VDT:** video display terminal **VRML:** virtual reality modeling language **WAP:** wireless application protocol **WEB TV:** the future of television, today, courtesy of Microsoft **WWW:** world wide web **XML:** extensible mark-up language; meta language describing content in terms of information formats being described

⋮

This book was designed at the Winter House Studio, Falls Village, Connecticut, by William Drenttel and Kevin Smith.

The typeface is Thesis, designed by Luc(as) de Groot in 1994.